THE PAI

N HALL

E PENINSULAR

AND THE SLUM

The Science of Police in

Victorian Durham

Michael McManus

Copyright © 2024 Michael McManus

All rights reserved.

ISBN: 9798872491002

For my Grandmother and Grandfather, Catherine and James McManus.

'Police' …. 'a whole cluster of practices and knowledge which are embedded at many points in the social field, and which constitute a set of policing structures encompassing *the whole of society*' (Pasquino 1978: 52).

CONTENTS

Acknowledgements   i

Preface   1

1 Introducing The Palatinate, The   6
   Peninsular and The Slum.

2 Theoretical Interpretation: The Science of   15
   Police, Moral Panic and Cultural Relic

3 The Palatinate: Irish Stereotyping, Crime   24
   and Disorder

4 The Peninsular   55

5 The Slum   63

6 Police of Crime and Disorder   76

7 Police of Public Utilities   114

8 Conclusions   140

9 Epilogue. Policing: From the Surveillance   149
   of Society to the Society of Surveillance

i

LIST OF TABLES

Table 1 Irish-born Population of County Durham 1841-1881, **38**

Table 2 Population of Durham City 1861, **39**

Table 3 Those charged before Durham City Petty Sessional Court 1856-1861, **41**

Table 4 Number of offences by type committed by Irish at Durham City Petty Sessional Court 1.1.1861-31.12.1861, **42**

Table 5 Population of County Durham 1871, **43**

Table 6 Irish defendants indicted before Durham Quarter Sessions 1867-1872, **44**

Table 7 Type and number of offences with which Irish charged Durham Quarter Sessions 1871, **45**

Table 8 Seven lowest areas of mortality by street, 1841-1851, **75**

Table 9 Seven highest areas of mortality by street 1841-1851, **118**

LIST OF FIGURES

Figure 1 The Stolen Altar Furniture, 3

Figure 2 Punch depicts and early species of Anarchic Celt, **35**

Figure 3 Respectable and loyal Irish assist the English police, **36**

Figure 4 William Robison Superintendent of Police 1848-57, **88**

Figure 5 Durham City Police Officers about 1850, **89**

The Palatinate, The Peninsular and The Slum

ACKNOWLEDGMENTS

I wish to thank the Committee of The North East Labour History Society who allowed me to re-use my articles here from North East History, Volume 32, 1988 and Northern Review, Volume 11, 2002.

PREFACE

It had been a crime of opportunity, and even in my
irreligious mind it conjured up the word 'sacrilege'. In
those heady days of the 1980's when churches went
unlocked, the thief had simply walked into St.
Oswald's Church and taken the solid silver altar
furniture - a crucifix and pair of candlesticks. As I
took details from the vicar to complete the crime
report and he told me about the connection between
the stolen goods and Durham City Police, I realized I
was historically implicated in this theft, and so too
were my other colleagues in that force. Normally,
arriving after the crime has taken place and to make

discoveries, detectives need to be time-travellers. But this investigation was to take me further back than the usual crime enquiry. As I began to take a further interest in the history of the Durham City Police and I extended my historical enquires, I would be travelling back to 1836.

On disbandment of the Durham City Borough Police in 1921, the uniforms of the officers were handed back to the Durham City Corporation. It is at this point that we can see the close association police had with the established church, which is so dominant in Durham City. The solid silver buttons from officer's tunics were melted down, recast as crucifix and candlesticks, and presented to clergy at St. Oswald's Church where they had remained until the thief removed them.

In 1980, the investigations to recover the silver items had taken officers to a scrap yard in industrial Tyneside where, hidden in the boot of an old car, the stolen silver artefacts were found relatively undamaged. The thief was arrested and later convicted. End of story? Well, not quite.

Figure 1. The Stolen Altar Furniture (Public Domain).

Time Travelling

As with my then current relationship with Durham City Police as a serving officer, my relationship with the Durham City Borough Police of the past continued. Fascinated by the fragment of history I had recovered and the need to know more about the early Durham City force, I visited the Durham County Record Office (DCRO). I was saddened to find that only a few accounts of the force had survived – a register of persons arrested and charged in 1863 and a couple of head constable's annual reports. In a sense, for me the destruction of the missing records was more serious than the theft of the church silver. Not just an artefact had been lost, but the irretrievable police discourse of an age. It was then that the enquiry widened.

One off-duty day I received information from a council workman which led me to the scene of another crime and on to the trail of another culprit. The culprit this time was Durham City Council. They had instructed workmen to clear rubbish from an old, abandoned building in Claypath. The building turned out to have once been the city police station. Several old documents had been found by workmen and they were instructed to take the books to the council incinerator to be burned. We will never know what was contained amongst these, for they were, indeed, reduced to ashes. One book, however, was secretly spared by a workman who had recognized its historical value. Written in the finest copperplate handwriting by members of the force, it was a rare register of 'beat complaints' made by residents of the

city between 1860 and 1871 (Hereafter, 'the register').
Knowing my interest in the subject the workman
offered the register to me. I gladly accepted of course.

It is from this register that I abstracted part of the
historical data for this book – the section on the
crime and disorder police. I was delighted with this
new-found historical resource, and to be involved for
a second time in preserving a fragment of the early
force's history. I deposited the register for safety at
police headquarters. Careful study of the register
revealed quite a lot about the culture of policing and
society in the city all those years ago.

1 INTRODUCING THE PALATINATE, THE PENINSULAR AND THE SLUM

This book explores a broad interpretation of policing and the police during the Victorian period in Durham County and City. It aims to encompass not only the concept of constabulary police but also a notion of police and policing linked to 'administration' in the nineteenth century. In doing so, the goal is for readers to grasp that police and policing involve more than just handling crime and disorder – police and policing can extend to many other powerful institutions and actors in the social realm. Here, 'administration' refers to the various policies, procedures, rules, and cultural shifts within society, involving state agents and institutions, beyond the notion of constabulary police. In this interpretation, for instance, we can understand the medical profession as 'police' controlling the medicalisation of society at times of social and cultural change.

To further prepare the reader, a brief description of the three concepts I use in the title of this book is provided - The Palatinate, The Peninsular and The Slum.

The Palatinate of County Durham

In England, Wales, and Ireland, a county palatine, or palatinate, was historically a region governed by a hereditary noble with unique authority and independence from the rest of the kingdom. The term originates from the Latin adjective '**palātīnus**' meaning 'relating to the palace' derived from the noun 'palātium' which means palace - in the case of Durham, its powerful Bishop, and his palace. It was the Bishop of Durham who had administered an army against the nearby Scottish to the north. In the 12th century, the Bishop of Durham held the highest rank among the bishops and barons. He presided over his own court and had nearly exclusive authority over his followers. Durham County had ten palatinate barons during this period, with notable families including the Hyltons of Hylton Castle, the Bulmers of Brancepeth, the Conyers of Sockburne, the Hansards of Evenwood, and the Lumleys of Lumley Castle. Additionally, the Neville family possessed significant estates in the county, notably Raby Castle.

Several structures associated with the bishops of Durham and the palatinate still exist, such as the castles in Durham and Norham, and the palace at Bishop Auckland, along with the exchequer building on Palace Green in Durham City. The current tourism industry frequently employs the term 'Land of the Prince Bishops'to showcase County Durham. This phrase is also visible on road signs upon entering County Durham unitary authority. The later history of the palatinate is characterised by the Crown and parliament slowly diminishing the powers of the bishops and incorporating the county into the regular system of local government in England. (Palatinate of Durham, Wikipedia).

The Peninsular of Durham City

The Peninsular in this book refers to the area of land in Durham City, almost surrounded by a body of water which is the River Wear, and which flows through Durham City from the Pennines in the west and eastward into the North Sea at Sunderland. This peninsular area consists primarily of Durham Cathedral, Durham Castle, Palace Green, The Baileys north and south, Saddler Street leading up to Owengate and, Dun Cow Lane. The area was historically created as a fortress against the Scottish, protecting the cathedral which houses the holy remains of St. Cuthbert. The Baileys are the location of several university colleges and many of the ecclesiastically residential buildings and houses of the better off. The Peninsular and its residents stand in stark contrast to the rest of the city, which has historically housed some of its poorest residents in slum and tenement buildings.

The Slum of Durham City

In the wider sense of the meaning for this study, The Slum could be defined as any other area than the Peninsular, however, that would preclude the fact that social and economic variation always existed in Durham society. Accordingly, to define it more precisely, I focus on a part of society and their dwelling areas representing the least well-off in the population. This allows recognition of the limited extent off the study and the need to manage it realistically. In view of this I have also concentrated on the Irish population, who, as immigrants in the mid 1800s, were categorically known as some of the poorest at the time and who were residing in the worst accommodation, for instance, tenements and houses in Framwellgate and Water Lane.

Theoretical Interpretation

Throughout book I use three theoretical devices to interpret the research findings. Firstly, Foucault's theory of discipline and surveillance in association with Pasquino's 'science of police' is used to observe the extent of the new administration of society which was occurring at the time. Secondly, in order to understand and assess how the immigrant Irish population were seen by the host nation, Cohen's 'Folk Devils and Moral Panics' is applied. Thirdly, Gidden's idea of De-Institutionalisation and 'Cultural Relic' is used at the end of the book to show how the present-day culture of policing has changed to quite a different level. These three devices are described in Chapter 2.

The Irish in Durham

In Chapter 3 I focus in detail on the Irish immigrants to Durham. They were a large and representative section of the working population of County Durham at the time and I will return to them in subsequent chapters. After 1840 the Irish consisted of a large proportion of the whole working class. They had arrived as immigrants from a catastrophic series of famines and resultant disease which had devastated their population. The Irish who settled in County Durham were amongst the poorest and least privileged in society and they were seen by many as 'them' rather than 'us' - as a large section of society may see immigrants in England today. The Irish were culturally and religiously different and they spoke differently, dressed differently, and, most importantly, they were historically seen as disloyal and dangerous to the British State. Accordingly, I examine the extent of Irish criminal behaviour and stereotyping in the media of the time and in court records.

The idea of 'Moral Panic' in sociology is about how the mass media, police, and community leaders might exaggerate and overreact to minor delinquent behaviour, both in terms of the type of offence and the number of people involved. This theory suggests that newspapers sometimes sensationalize small social events, but the consequences can be more significant, leading to calls for harsh social penalties on the group being targeted. Using this theory, I want to explore how the media in mid-nineteenth century Durham might have created the stereotype of the Durham Irish as socially deviant.

In Chapters 4 and 5 a topographical, social, and economic description is provided of two opposing Durham City communities - The Peninsular and The Slum. Some caution is needed here. The cultural change during the early period of this study on the existence of social boundaries, especially between the capitalist and working classes, is not an easy one to describe. In recognizing the need to show the social boundaries existing in nineteenth century Durham society it must be remembered that all social systems are complex, therefore, using polar categories, such as 'rich' and 'poor', to determine the class characteristics of a population ignores the complexity of a society and does no justice to accuracy. This can also be seen in singularly placing various categories of occupation, such as 'labourer' and 'tradesman', under one conceptual scheme. An accurate assessment would require an understanding far in advance of the analysis I give here. In using the opposites of 'haves' and 'have-nots', and in focusing on samples of the population, such as the Irish and residents of the Peninsular Parishes, I therefore accept that a truly accurate picture of social division is impossible in this study. In view of this, I use these categories merely to provide a general understanding of the diversity of social class in Durham City.

Chapters 6 and 7 relate to the two forms of police and policing which, both comprise the interpretation of the 'science of police' in this study. The Police of Crime and Disorder and The Police of Public Utilities are merged to demonstrate the new administrative culture which was taking place.

Chapter 8 brings together the previous chapters and an overall analysis is offered. This is followed by a prologue in which I make some comments on 'then and now' comparisons of police culture by introducing some contemporary cultural phase-changes, and pose the question, what has really changed?

2 THEORETICAL INTERPRETATION: THE SCIENCE OF POLICE, MORAL PANIC AND CULTURAL RELIC

In a century of great cultural, social, and industrial change, an overwhelming amount of policy and procedure relating to regulation, enforcement, and sanction, existed in the daily lives of nineteenth century Britons. If we take Durham City as an example and consider crime and disorder as well as the administration of public health, we discover an immense number of references to the governance of public behaviour by institutions and administrators which impacted greatly on the population of the city and on its culture in a wide range of areas.

The New Administration: The Science of Police

Here I want to convey and define policing and police in association with 'administration' in nineteenth century Durham. Building on Foucault's ideas (Foucault, 1975), Pasquino convincingly argues that during this time and throughout the nineteenth century, culture was heavily influenced by what he calls the 'science of police' (Pasquino, 1978). However, it is important to note that when Pasquino refers to 'police' he isn't just talking about the regular law enforcement. Instead, he wants us to grasp 'police' or 'administration' in a more nuanced and broader sense, encompassing, numerous practices and knowledge which are woven into various aspects of the social landscape, forming a network of policing structures that extend across the entirety of society (ibid: 52). Foucault's and Pasquino's scrutiny of the development of disciplinary society yields insights into the factors facilitating an administrative transformation across all institutions within Durham society.

With the introduction of Sir Robert Peel's 'New Police' system in 1829, the criminal justice system was ramping-up its administration around this period with the objective of improving effectiveness and efficiency in the control of people and their daily lives. For instance, in the public's leisure pursuits in streets, on water and their obstruction of highways and offences of begging and vagrancy, all of which were regularly prosecuted by the constabulary police of the new Durham City force, inaugurated in 1836.

When it comes to environmental matters in public health, such as sewage, buildings, roads, and pavements, 240 references to Durham City Council Paving Commissioners' minutes, accounts, and other correspondence, can be found in records from 1790 to 1850 in Durham County Record Office (DCRO). The Council Paving Commissioners were the administrative body legally responsible for managing these areas.

What interested Foucault was the relation between the state and the population, where technology, power, and knowledge are inseparable. From documentary evidence, and discourses relating to the regulation of society in nineteenth century public institutions, Foucault's rendering of history makes it clear that institutions were being used to strengthen social relations and ensure that society was properly ordered. A potent example here is the Victorian prison. Other than they held prisoners within them Zedner reminds us that:

> They also provided strong prudential reasons for self-discipline, restraint, and conformity among the working poor, who were anxious to remain outside their walls (Zedner, 2009: 32).

There are several powerful architectural images in Durham City; the cathedral, and the Victorian prison are just two. As a resident of Durham City for most of my life I know that being in the area around Durham Prison and outside its walls reminds me of my freedom and the need to remain outside, not inside its walls. The sight of the prison has that strong effect on most people's feelings and thoughts.

The move towards cultural change had begun earlier than the appearance of Durham Prison, in the eighteenth century. In terms of time, Foucault argues that an historical shift occurred from a sovereignty based on a bloody exercise of power over citizens' bodies ('the right to death') to one that emerged around 1700, based on the *regulation of the population and the disciplining of the individual* ('the power over life').

As noted earlier, when Pasquino talks of 'police' he is not simply talking about the constabulary police. Rather, he wants us to understand 'police', or alternatively, 'administration', in a more sophisticated and wider sense, relative to:

> …. a whole cluster of practices and knowledge which are embedded at many points in the social field, and which constitute a set of policing structures encompassing *the whole of society* (ibid: 52).

Here we see a model of societal change wherein the 'science of police' was the consequence of the breakdown of feudalism and the consequent search for new ways of conceiving social order – an interpretation absolutely germane to the present study.

Surveillance

Pasquino argues that this change was necessary because of the perceived threat to social order, especially posed by the newly emerging class of poverty, which we observe in the present study. We can easily see the Irish population as part of this perceived threat to order. The objective of scientific policing was the prosperity of the state through a perpetual surveillance of the population and the threat of sanction. Accordingly, 'the science of police' becomes a means of managing the poor, and others who threaten the status quo of social order. In effect, a dominant culture as, *management of the population* exists (Kendall and Whickham, 1999). Drawing upon this method of analysis, I seek here to demonstrate a synthesis between Foucault's theoretical position and empirical data from the public records of nineteenth century Durham City; both criminal justice and public health records. I do this with Pasquino's idea of a broader definition of policing and police.

Them and Us

According to Foucault, culture as management is linked to the process of growth and the establishment of capitalist dominance over target populations. And the poor, and those who threaten the security of the state are principal targets of surveillance by state actors. Thus, the social landscape is comprised of diverse *groups* having social and economic categories at varying levels (Williams, 1983: 60-69). For the purposes of identification, these can be appropriately labelled as Bourgeoisie; those having 'economic production power', and Proletariat; those having a 'revolutionary labour power'; terms used by Marx and Engels. For them, Bourgeoisie describes the class who are *owners of the means of production* while Proletariat refers to *a revolutionary working class* under capitalism, which, according to the British State, included the Irish nation and its population.

For academic purposes here, these categories were quite distinguishable in nineteenth century Durham City. The coming of industrialization in the nineteenth century, and the associated population increase amongst the poorer classes in areas like Durham, created social, cultural, and religious polarization between the established order and the working classes. This polarization and diversity was reflected in specific areas of the city, as will be outlined in detail in coming chapters.

Moral Panic

The sociological concept of Moral Panic refers to the alleged overreaction of the mass media, police, and local community leaders to delinquency, which is trivial, both in terms of the nature of the offence and the number of people involved. The theory suggests that newspapers indulge in sensationalism by exaggerating trivial social events, but the effects may be more serious, resulting in calls for severe social penalties on the target population. Using the immigrant Irish population to Durham in the mid 1800s, I put this theory to the test.

Cultural Relic

Cultural Relic is part of Giddens' overall theory of Reflexive Modernization, and the De-institutionalisation of society. Giddens argues that in the modern era, society is being democratised in every way. Many symbols of the so-called 'Golden Age' of traditional policing and health services have become a memory - locked away like 'Relics' in a 'living museum' of policing and health provision. Importantly, he argues that, despite this, many areas of these traditional services, especially in cultural matters, do not go away (Giddens, 1971, 1987, Giddens, Beck and Lash, 1994). Using my contemporary experiences as a serving police officer, in the final Prologue, I provide some observations of this claim and see if this theory can hold sway.

In the next chapter I consider the extent to which the stereotype of the Durham Irish as socially deviant was created by the media and calculate the occurrence of crime and disorder by the Irish population.

3 THE PALATINATE: IRISH STEREOTYPING, CRIME AND DISORDER

Applying the theory of Moral Panic mentioned in the previous chapter, I seek here to ascertain the extent to which the stereotype of the Durham Irish as socially deviant was created by the media of mid-nineteenth century Durham. Similar studies, carried out of the Irish in York (Finnigan, 1986: 59-84), Wolverhampton (Swift, 1986: 5-29) and London (Feheney, 1983: 319-329) during this period have provided evidence to support the theory. Cooter's research on this theory in Durham, however, does not support the theory (Cooter, 1972).

The research method used here consisted of comparing newspaper reports with court records to identify variations in reporting patterns, which may indicate prejudice and moral panic in relation to the Irish population. The newspaper data were obtained from newspaper reports between the years 1861 and 1871. To obtain a general view of criminality in 1861 I used the Durham City Petty Sessional Court records of that year since they contain details of the bulk of criminal activity in the Durham area which came to the notice of the police and led to a prosecution. It should be noted, however, that police statistics are an unreliable measure of the volume of crime, as only a small proportion of the actual crime rate is reported to the police. Those Irish who appeared before this court were seventeen years of age and above and would have consisted of native-born Irish immigrants who had fled times of famine in Ireland after 1847. Comparisons of these records were made primarily with reports on Irish matters from the weekly Durham County Advertiser of 1861.

To assess the Irish involvement in more serious crime, court records from Durham County Quarter Sessions between 1867 and 1872 were also examined. Articles relating to the Irish from the Durham Chronicle of 1871 were compared with these records. The Durham Chronicle, also a weekly newspaper, reported on a wider geographical area of County Durham than did the Durham County Advertiser and included news from Gateshead, Darlington, Bishop Auckland, Durham City, Stockton, Sunderland, and West Hartlepool. Each issue of these newspapers was scanned during the year in question and all data referring to the Irish were abstracted and analysed.

Were immigrant Durham Irish significantly more criminal than the host population? If so, how can this be explained, or were the local media exaggerating the situation and in doing so creating a moral panic? Stereotyping the Irish, however, has its origins in a much earlier periods of history. In order, therefore, to set the scene clearly for the Durham research it is first appropriate to consider the roots of the subject in question in a geographically wider context.

The Irish Folk Devil

Native Irish had an obvious distrust of foreign invaders to Ireland. An old Irish proverb, author unknown, warns:

> Beware the hoof of the horse, the horn of the bull and the smile of the Saxon.

This was aggravated by the invader's perception that the Irish were barbarians - indeed, the contrast between civilization and barbarism has been a continuing theme in world history (Jones, 1971: xii-1). In the eleventh century, for instance, the powerful Anglo-Normans encountered many Celtic tribal societies during their process of settlement in Ireland. From this time the familiar derogatory images of the Irish as inferior, barbarous, primitive, savage and indolent were created by foreign settlers. Later Tudor settlers in Ireland arrived with preconceived ideas of the Irish and, despite contradictory evidence, they fashioned the host community to fit these preconceived stereotypes (Canny, 1973: 30-34). This legend of the Irish as inferior, barbarous savages has grown up over the centuries. Legendary mists are notoriously hard to disperse.

In developing their own system of values, powerful settlers in Ireland were able to impose their values on the less powerful and they labelled those who infringed their rules as 'deviants'. Acts can be defined as deviant in particular societies at times for particular reasons. Deviance is therefore a relative concept, not an absolute category. It is possible in many versions of this theory that the criminal is a victim of the criminal justice system. And there is much evidence to show that the powerful settlers in Ireland did impose their dominant values upon the native Irish:

> They ….. regarded the Irish as later colonists looked upon the Red Indians - as being like wild beast, beyond the pale of the moral law (Lecky 1982: 1).

Several other writers have shown how the native Irish were victims of the criminal justice system. Analogies have been made with the 'villein' in England at the same period (Richardson, 1938: 382-393; Otway-Ruthven, 1950: 1-16). A distinct alien status, therefore, was applied to the Irish in their own country. No better evidence can be found for this than around the time of the twelfth century when there existed a defence in law to the charge of killing an Irishman unlawfully. If it could be shown that the deceased was 'Homo et Nativus' of a named Irish lord acquittal would follow and financial compensation would be made to the lord (Northern Irish Law Quarterly, vol. 23, 1972: 417).

For a period before, and several years after the Irish Rebellion of 1641, some communities in England, especially in the West Country, were uneasy owing to anticipated attacks on their homes and institutions by Papists and Irish:

> Among foreigners the most feared were the Irishmen and their presence (usually as migrants looking for work) could occasionally trigger-off local panics (Lindley, 1972: 144).

Beggars and the unemployed were blamed for carrying much rumour about these attacks. The Privy

Council of the time reported that there were many false rumours, and these distracted the people's minds. Much of the rumour, however, was effected by persons in positions of officialdom and responsibility. For instance, a panic in Colchester in June 1640 arose, at least in part, from the mayor's willingness to credit an allegation made by children. An armed skirmish between Catholics and Protestants in Lancashire resulted directly from the Mayor of Chester's Anti-Catholic precautions. Prominence was also given to Irish matters in tract material throughout the crucial months after the Irish Rebellion and the English public were kept fully informed of matters in Ireland through these tracts. It may be difficult to ascertain how true or false these media reports were but there is no doubting the repercussions they produced. In modern terms, more 'crime-control-oriented decisions' (Hall, 1978) occurred in the form of the confiscations of the Cromwellian land settlement in Ireland. A parliamentary army took the opportunity to wreak vengeance upon the Irish, even in England. Prisoners judged to be Irish were hanged or drowned. These kinds of retribution were most common in the West of England where the threat was geographically closest (Clifton,1984: 155-156).

Such conclusions as are described above allude to a theory of Folk Devils and Moral Panics (Cohen, 1980) for the structural and cultural position of the Irish, together with their firm denial of Protestantism, was portrayed as a deviant action and style. Social reaction soon becomes involved with elements of misperception of the problem. It is not unreasonable to presume that these misperceptions, and the resultant images created by a distortion of reality, may have relevance to fairness of justice. Fear of Catholics and their association with Ireland supplied the basis of the popular political vocabulary of the time. So, it was not surprising that both moral and physical panics did occur. Such events would probably have qualified and perpetuated the traditional Irish stereotype. These derogatory images of the Irish could still be traced in the Victorian period:

> The Irish child can dance a jig,
> And share a pillow with a pig,
> And when we ask for pie or meat,
> The pratie he is glad to eat (Lucas, 1925: 6).

31

Scientific racism was popular in the mid-nineteenth century. Such a dogma requires a belief that humanity is divided into unchanging natural types, recognizable by physical features, and that mental and moral behaviour also relates to physical features. Accordingly, proponents of this theory argued that it is race that determines individual and natural behaviour - including criminality. In the popular periodicals of the time the working classes of the mid-nineteenth century were bombarded with material relating to these beliefs:

> The Jewish hawk nose indicates considerable shrewdness in worldly matters, a deep insight into character and facility for turning this insight to profitable account, the Irish snub nose indicates natural weakness, mean, disagreeable disposition ... petty insolence and divers other characteristics of conscious weakness (Lloyds Weekly Miscellany, 1849-1850: 823).

So, instead of the view that institutions and traditions may well have determined the nature of the criminal, the notion that the nature of the criminal determined the character of institutions and traditions was a popular belief (Lombroso, 1876). This was the period which followed the rise of Darwinism (Darwin, 1871).

Periodicals of the time required the working classes to believe that the Irish:

> Driven from their own proper locality into certain widely different districts of the country, had not only degenerated in their general bodily conformation, but have actually acquired the prognathous or Negro type of cranium (Working-Man's Friend, 5 January 1850: 10).

Anti-Celtic racism can be seen in Punch cartoons of the time. The Celt is often depicted as a gorilla standing at the bottom of the evolutionary tree. In contrast, loyal Celts would be depicted with Grecian purity of feature, for instance the figure of Hibernia herself (Gilley and Swift,1986: 5).

The Victorians even claimed a connection between Catholicism and crime (Ragged School Union Magazine, 1854: 104). Bearing in mind that ninety per cent of the Catholic population in such areas as London were Irish, it would not be unreasonable to assume that the Victorians' claim had in mind Irish Catholics of the lower class (Feheney, op.cit.: 20). It is argued that the notions of moral panics and deviancy amplification were born from this idea that the media and others, such as the police, who can influence society, suggest, and promote a selective view of deviance (Cohen, op. cit.). Perhaps, however, it should not be overlooked that, conversely, the stereotype already to be found in popular opinion may have influenced what found its way into print. Just how seriously the public is influenced by derogatory images is important for equity in criminal justice, for the stereotype of the wild Irishman, drunken, violent, dishonest, and dirty, is probably not readily exchanged by some for a more realistic image.

Figure 2. Punch depicts an early species of Anarchic
Celt threatening the young girl Hibernia, protected by
Britannia (Gilley, 1985:21).

Figure 3. Respectable and loyal Irish assist the English Police in the battle against the Fenians (Gilley, ibid).

The image of the Irishman was always a source of amusement in Victorian newspapers and periodicals, and stereotypes develop over the years as a combination of ignorance, propaganda, humour, history, and hearsay. For instance, in Durham, as elsewhere, the Irish were distinctive and noticeable with their strange appearance and dress, brogue and customs, and they were often singled out from the rest of the community. A report, headed 'Ireland for the Irish', on a public meeting held in Durham City Town Hall in 1861 to discuss the repeal of the Union, clearly shows this tendency to stereotype:

> The audience being almost entirely composed of Irish residents of this City and surrounding districts, the garb and general exterior of whom were unmistakable evidence as to the land of their nativity (Durham County Advertiser, 18.1.1861).

Thus, the deep-seated frictions between the Irish and the host community were often released in less dramatic ways than violence. But what evidence was there of this theory in County Durham newspapers?

Owing to its massive industrial base and demand for labour, County Durham in Victorian times had been a popular location for Irish immigrants escaping poverty and disease in their own island during the Irish Famine, primarily 1847-1850. This was at the height of the Industrial Revolution, which had not really affected Ireland to any extent and, conveniently, the industrial Northeast of England was a welcoming

relief for the Irish immigrants. As seen in Table 1,
County Durham had a high proportion of Irish-born
in its population and, furthermore, a higher such
proportion in its population in 1861 than any other
English county, excluding Lancashire, Cheshire, and
Cumberland (Norris, 1984: 71).

Table 1

Irish-born Population of County Durham 1841-1881

Year	Number	% of total
1841	5407	1.6
1851	18501	4.5
1861	27719	5.4
1871	37515	5.5
1881	36794	4.2

(Census' of England and Wales).

In addition, towards the height of this pattern of
immigration it can be seen from Table 2 that in 1861
the percentage of the Irish-born population of
Durham City was also very high.

Table 2
Population of Durham City, 1861

	Number	% of total
Population		
English-born	12720	90.2
Irish-born	898	6.4
Scottish-born	398	2.9
Remainder	72	0.5
Total	14088	

(1861 Census of England and Wales, Vol.15: 160).

Court Records

Table 3 shows the extent of Irish criminality compared with that of the rest of the population of Durham City between 1856 and 1861. Irish-related crime was comparatively low; it was, however, disproportionate to the community's size. There is a predominance of Irish drunkenness and disorderliness, violence-related offences, and theft. It is interesting to note that 50% of the theft cases were dismissed by the Durham Magistrates. What is more striking is the fact that 10.5% of the Irish population of Durham City were involved in criminality during the year 1861. In contrast, the non-Irish population was 50% less criminal - only 5% were criminally involved. While there were some cases of theft, which could be associated with severe social need, for instance the theft of clothing, in the main the type of property stolen did not particularly indicate any notion of a basic need for survival on behalf of the offender. The data show no evidence of high rates of Irish vagrant crime, and this compares favourably with other similar research (Jones op. cit.).

Table 3

Those Charged before Durham City Petty Sessional Court between 1856-1861

Period	Defendants		% of total
15.10.1856 - 4.6.1857	Irish	19	9.0
	Other	189	81.0
1.7.1859 -13.12.1859	Irish	15	4.3
	Other	337	95.7
1.1.1860 - 31.12.1860	Irish	32	4.3
	Other	704	95.7
1.1.1861 - 31.12.1861	±Irish	95	12.4
	*Other	669	87.6

*(5.0% of that population)
±(10.5% of that population)

(Durham County Record Office (DCRO):
PS/DU/1/2: Durham Petty Sessional Court charge book, 1856-1862).

The variety and type of offences with which Irish defendants were charged before Durham City Petty Sessional Court are shown in Table 4.

Table 4

Number of Offences by Type committed by Irish and heard at Durham City Petty Sessional Court between 1.1.1861 and 31.12.1861.

Robbery with violence	1
Larceny	12
Assaulting PC in execution of his duty	3
Assault	7
Threats to assault	4
Aggravated assault on female	1
Drunk and disorderly	36
Drunkenness	10
Drunk and indecent	3
Prostitution	1
Brawling	6
Aiding and abetting brawling	1
Vagrancy	1
Begging	1
Wilful damage	3
Drive furiously	1
Nuisance	4
Against Lodging House Act	1
Misdemeanour	2
Total	98

(DCRO, PS/DH1/2: Durham Petty Sessional Court charge book, 1856-1862).

The more serious criminal-offence charges were considered for the year 1871 and are shown in Table 5. This year saw the highest ever Irish-born population in County Durham.

Table 5

Population of County Durham, 1871

		% of total population
Irish-born	37515	5.5
Other	647574	94.5

(Census of England and Wales, Vol.16:100 and Vol.18: 541).

Table 6 shows a steady increase in serious crime committed by Irish persons. This increase runs parallel to the numerical increase in the Irish population between 1867 and 1872.

Table 6

Irish Defendants Indicted before Durham Quarter Sessions, 1867-1872

Year	Total Offenders	Irish	Irish as % of total population
1867	198	16	8.0
1868	169	16	9.5
1869	227	29	12.8
1870	234	34	14.5
1871	202	30	14.9
1872	286	45	15.7
Total	1316	170	12.9

(DCRO, Q/S/C1: Durham County Quarter Sessions calendar of prisoners, 1867-1872).

As criminals the Irish were well outnumbered by the rest of the community - on average between 1867 and 1872 for every 87 others indicted there were thirteen Irish. As can be seen by analysis of Tables 5 and 6, however, the Irish contribution to serious crime was greatly disproportionate to the numbers in that community. Furthermore, it can be seen that some 0.07% of the Irish population of Durham County were involved in serious crime in 1871. In contrast, the non-Irish population, at 0.03%, were at least 50% less criminal than the Irish. One third of the Irish indicted in 1871 had previously served terms of imprisonment - some many times. Those who had been imprisoned on previous occasions accounted for 33% of the total Irish defendants at Quarter Sessions. An analysis of the type and number of serious offences charged at Quarter Sessions in 1871 is shown in Table 7.

Table 7

Type and Number of Offences with which Irish were charged at Durham Quarter Sessions in 1871

Riot	3
Wounding	9
Assault with intent to steal	1
Burglary	1
Larceny.	16
Total	30

(DCRO, Q/S/C1: Durham County Quarter Sessions calendar of prisoners, 1867-1872).

Fenianism and Disorder

The absence of any entry in the register of incidents relating to industrial and political unrest in Durham City is supported to some extent in the local newspapers of the time, however, some incidents did occur.

The 1860's was a time in which the Irish population, at home and abroad, were deeply unhappy about the Act of Union between England and Ireland. A repeal of the act was on the agenda of many in the Irish community in the North East. On the evening of Monday, 14th. January 1861 a large public meeting took place in Durham City Town Hall in furtherance of the repeal of the union, and many Irish people attended. The long proceedings were recorded in detail by a local newspaper reporter who, by the tone of his writing, appeared to have a clear dislike for the Irish:

> …. the audience being almost entirely composed of Irish residents of this city and surrounding districts, the garb and general exterior of whom were unmistakable evidence as to the land of their nativity………. (Durham County Advertiser,18.1.1861.).

The Irish working-class were closely monitored by the police during this period and the large Irish population in County Durham at that time was certainly a cause of concern for the Durham County Constabulary. The police showed a particular interest in the Irish community because of a popular perception by them, and indeed many ordinary citizens, that Irish immigrants had a propensity towards criminality (Swift, 1984: 87-108; Swift, 1986: 5-29). This is borne out by working-class weekly newspapers of the time (Paz, 1986).

More particularly, political violence by the Irish was a worrying factor for the police. This concern is reflected in local Orders of the time issued by Lieutenant Colonel George Francis White, the Chief Constable of the Durham County Constabulary. The tone of these orders would have been influenced by the Chief Constable's regular contact with the Home Office and the overall national picture concerning the problem of Fenianism. On 19th. October 1867 Lieutenant Colonel White had written a confidential memorandum to Superintendents, set out here in full:

In accordance with the tenor of the confidential circular from the Home Office, dated 28th. September, 1867, and which was read to the Divisional Superintendents assembled at Head Quarters, (sic) the Chief Constable directs that each Superintendent will tell off a sufficient number of sergeants or other discreet and intelligent men in his division whose duty it will be to watch, for the present, the Irish population, and report without delay through him to the Chief Constable, any information they may obtain of Fenian organisation or suspicious movements or persons, such duty to be conducted in such a manner as, if possible, not to attract attention, and the information kept secret. Superintendents will report to the Chief Constable immediately any information of importance they receive in addition to a monthly report in writing as to the state of the Irish population. By authority from the Secretary of State and Justices of the County, the Chief Constable has issued to each Superintendent of the force a limited number of revolver pistols with proportionate ammunition, holsters and pouches, not to be used by the police on ordinary duty, but only entrusted to select constables in cases of emergency or when employed on service of personal danger. The Superintendents will be held responsible for the custody of these arms, which, as well as cutlasses will, until further orders be kept secure in a chest or other safe place under lock and key but separate from the ammunition (Durham County Constabulary General Order Book. DCRO, Ref. CCP 32: 211).

The police had good cause to be forearmed. Several riots between the Irish and English inhabitants of County Durham had already taken place in the years prior to this Order being published. For instance, in 1858 public disorder as the result of disharmony between the Irish and English communities had occurred at Consett. Reports of this, and other disturbances of the time, are clearly recorded relating to the county police force (Durham County Constabulary, Chief Constable's Reports of 1859. DCRO, Ref. CCP). Yet no serious Irish problems appeared to exist in Durham City. Apart from the odd Irish brawl in Framwellgate, it is almost as if the city area was cocooned from such matters.

The Media

Irish matters were mentioned sixteen times in the *Durham County Advertiser* in 1861. Two types of report were evident, Irish jokes and Irish brawls, examples of which follow:

> A Scot and an Irishman thrashing for a Dutch farmer in America, the former observed to the latter that in the course of a long residence in this country he had remarked the uncommon docility of the horses that among many instances of their tractability he had actually seen them employed in thrashing the wheat. 'Arrah my jewel' cried Pat 'I'm half a dozen years too ripe to believe that'. The Scot persisted that what he had said was true, and Pat, staggered at length by his serious and repeated assertations *(sic)*, exclaimed in tones of wonder 'And how do the horses hold the flails?'

(Durham County Advertiser, 29 March 1861).

> An Irish foreman to a stevedore discharging a ship's cargo to India required some extra help on deck so he went to the hatchway and shouted down the hold to the men working there, 'Now then, how many of you down there is there? 'Three of us' was the reply. 'Then come up here the half of you directly', says the foreman.

(Durham County Advertiser, 5 July 1861).

> Patrick Margan, an old Irish piper, a regular visitor at Durham during the hiring's, charged with drunk and disorderly.

(Durham County Advertiser, 10 May 1861).

> Thomas Digny, Patrick Docherty and Patrick Barratt, three Irish Drainers living at Brandon, brawling. Docherty and Digny found stripped and fighting at the top of Parsons Field. Barratt aided and abetted -- the next morning he was making peace between them, after encouraging them previously. The Mayor said it was disgraceful conduct for a Sunday.

(Durham County Advertiser, 19 July 1861).

Apart from several of these reports, however, there was no reporting in the Durham County Advertiser which specifically overemphasized Irish criminality or an Irish propensity to committing particular offences. It would appear, therefore, that even if the media were aware of the disproportion of Irish criminality to the Irish population, they did not wish openly to draw the public's attention to it. This is contrary to the evidence presented in similar studies in York

(Finnigan, op. cit.), Wolverhampton (Swift, op. cit.) and London (Feheney, op. cit.) but the present findings do tend to support the conclusions of another local study of County Durham (Cooter, 1972).

Although there were no data found in the Durham County Advertiser which directly exaggerated the criminality of the Irish there were several pieces, such as the jokes shown above, which implied the Irish were simple-minded. When this tendency is taken in conjunction with other articles in the newspaper, there is an impression given that native English were mentally superior to the Irish. This conclusion concurs with other research findings (Paz, 1986: 613).

There were fourteen mentions of Irish matters in the Durham Chronicle of 1871. Again, no imbalance concerning Irish criminality was discovered in these, although half of the reports described offences of violence. For instance, a serious stabbing at West Hartlepool:

> Irish stabbed Irish. The Superintendent spoke in strong terms as to the brutality constantly exercised by the Irish towards one another on account of jealousies engendered by secret societies. (Durham Chronicle, 30.6.1871.).

> Extraordinary proceedings at a christening: alleged cutting and wounding at Spennymoor. Three Irishmen accused of wounding of father at his child's christening at Spennymoor. There were signs of those present having indulged too freely on the bottle......one used improper language to a young woman and caused the argument preceding the violence. (ibid).

In contrast to the Durham County Advertiser, I found no direct derogatory remarks on Irish mentality in the Durham Chronicle.

The Durham Chronicle did report a serious incident between Irishmen. Durham Spring Assizes heard evidence in 1851 of disorder and violence caused at Witton Park, near Crook, by men from the Irish counties of Monaghan and Galway. Matthew Martin, 30 years, John Mahon, 22 years, Patrick Grant, 24 years, Philip Martin, 22 years, John Griffin, 23 years and Patrick McGough, 26 years had violently assaulted George Hart, with intent to do him grievous bodily harm. Hart was a local police officer and on 28th. September 1850, he had been called to a public house where revelry had advanced to riot and one of the party had been wounded. The officer, after ejecting some of the persons, was proceeding to seek a surgeon for the wounded man when he was struck with a poker across his face and immediately afterwards was knocked down by a blow from behind. While on the ground the officer was kicked and seriously injured. The assault was so severe that P.C. Hart lost an eye. He later gave evidence that it was one of the Martins' who had struck him with the poker. During the same incident another officer was also seriously assaulted and rendered insensible by a savage attack from the Irishmen. A poker and iron spit were produced as being the probable weapons. All except Grant were found guilty and each was sentenced to two years imprisonment, which they saw out in Durham Jail (Durham Chronicle, 14.3.1851).

Although there was no direct and obvious overemphasis on Irish criminality in the Durham media there was an overall tendency to identify Irish nationality when reporting incidents of lawlessness. This contrasted with the non-Irish reports, where specific nationality remained unidentified. Furthermore, I was unable to find even one report which praised the Irish. The Durham Chronicle tended to give special attention to reports of Irish violence occurring elsewhere than in County Durham. In view of these reporting tendencies, it is reasonable to conclude that, although a moral panic was not evident, Ireland and the Irish were being stereotyped in a negative and discreditable fashion.

4 THE PENINSULAR

The purpose of this chapter is to determine the type of society and social class residing in the Peninsular of Durham City, which area comprises the cathedral, castle, and Baileys and surrounds. It has always been an important social and religious landmark - symbolizing economic power and righteousness. Its natural boundary, and proximity to the rest of the city, provides the potential to effectively block the establishment of human relations and social contacts. Indeed, this was its fortress-like purpose in earlier times.

The former monks of Lindisfarne had occupied the Peninsular of Durham as a resting place for St. Cuthbert's body seventy years before the Norman Conquest. As well as a place to build a cathedral in his memory, the Peninsular was a key defence of the border with Scotland. Some fortifications were built early in the eleventh century on the site of the present castle to add to the natural defences the peninsular provided. The loss of this area to Scotland would have surely been an economic disaster for the English crown. The Prince Bishops of Durham were, therefore, involved in the dual role of exercising both religious and military/economic governance on behalf of the monarch. Thus, the Durham Peninsular as, '......half church of God, half castle against the Scot........' is an appropriate statement:

> Grey Towers of Durham yet well I love thy mixed and massive piles, half church of God, half castle against the Scot, and long to roam these venerable isles, with records of deeds long since forgot (Sir Walter Scot).

The population of the Peninsular Parishes in 1851 was 513. Within the peninsular we could calculate the number of servants in an area as representing the existence, or otherwise, of a bourgeois community. If this is undertaken in the Peninsular Parishes, it is not surprising to discover a large servant class. In 1851 Saint Mary the Less Parish consisted of seventeen inhabited dwellings in South Bailey. Here there were 45 persons categorized as servants. St. Mary-le-Bow Parish consisted of sixty inhabited dwellings comprising of North Bailey, Hatfield Hall, Bow Lane, Dun Cow Lane, and Queen Street and here there were eighty-one servants. College consisted of twelve inhabited dwellings where forty-seven servants resided. Castle and Precincts, and houses adjoining South Bailey, consisted of the Old Grammar School, Queen Street, Library, Castle, one house in Saddler Street, Banks Cottage, Museum and Garden Cottage. Here there were ten servants.

In this census a total of 513 persons are named in these parishes, of which all were English born, apart from one Italian, two Scots, two Welsh and three Irish. These three Irish persons were not servants and comprised two students and one visitor. 173 of the totals were categorized as servants, specifically house servants, domestic, cooks, gardeners, grooms, ladies' maids, governess, housemaids, butlers, nurses and footmen and footboys. All the servants were born in English counties, 108 of whom were born in County Durham. The Durham Directory of 1851 provides us with some information on buildings and inhabitants of these parishes. If we consider as examples College, Palace Green, Queen Street and South Bailey it is possible to characterize the residents clearly as socially and economically privileged.

Peninsular Residents

At *College* were Reverend Temple Chevallier, BD; Venerable Archdeacon Raymond DD; The Very Reverend George Waddington DD (Dean); Reverend George Townsend DD; Reverend J. Edwards MA; Reverend Henry Jenkyns DD; Reverend W.S. Gilly DD; Venerable Archdeacon Thorpe DD; Reverend Henry Douglas MA; Reverend David Durell DD; Reverend J.S. Ogle DD; Samuel Rowlandson Esq.; William Hartley, Porter and Verger. Residing in the *Palace Green* were, Robert Burrell Esq.; Misses Burrell; John Moore, Verger; Mrs. Jones, Abbey Churchyard. In *Queen Street* were, Maynard and Middleton,

Solicitors; Bishop's Alms-houses; William Howe, Joiner; Mr. Newby, Plumber, and Gas Fitter: T. Rushward, Carver and Gilder; John W. Hayes, Solicitor; George Moor, Solicitor; Subscription News Rooms; Subscription Library; Charles Reed, Newsagent. Premises and occupants in *South Bailey* included Matthew Woodfield Esq.; Mrs. Wilson; John Church Backhouse, Banker; Mrs. G.T. Fox; Reverend G.T. Fox MA; Mrs. Blackburn; Joseph Davison, Solicitor; Miss Stuart, Boarding School; Mrs. T. Greenwell; Henry Greenwell, Solicitor; Edward Shippardson Esq.; Mrs. Shields; Mr. Hastings, Artist; William Charles Chaytor, Solicitor; Miss Chaytor; Walter Scruton, Solicitor; Reverend H. Walford MA.

Case Study

The foregoing list of residents provides a very clear picture of the social class residing in the peninsular. If we take an individual case study and consider John Backhouse as one resident, we get an even stronger interpretation of the social class living there (McCollum, 1973; Banham, 1994).

John Church Backhouse (1811-1858) was born into Darlington's great Quaker banking family. He also had a family home at Blackwell, Darlington. His father was John Backhouse; his mother was Eliza (née Church, a military family from County Cork, Ireland). His sister Eliza married into the world-renowned Barclay banking family. John Church Backhouse was a descendent of John and Sarah Backhouse, members of the Society of Friends in Yealand Redmayne, Lancashire about 1660. His brother, Jonathan Backhouse junior, inherited the family fortunes on the death of their father in 1826. By the end of the 18th century the family had established itself in Darlington, County Durham, first as linen manufacturers and then as bankers with expanding business interests, and the family had allied itself by marriage with the Peases', Darlington's most prominent Quaker family.

The banking firm, known until 1798 as, James and Jonathan Backhouse and Co., was started in 1774 by Jonathan Backhouse, who married Ann Pease. James was Jonathan's younger brother. On the former's death in 1826 control passed to his son, Jonathan

Backhouse junior (1779-1842), who in 1811 had married Hannah Chapman (1787-1850), eldest daughter of Joseph Gurney, Quaker, and banker, of Lakenham Grove, Norfolk.

Ties of kinship established with the Barclay, Birkbeck, Chapman, Church, Fox, Hoare, and Hodgkin families consolidated the Backhouses' position in the country's Quaker banking and business network (McCollum, 1973). The great economic power of the Backhouse family was substantial because they:

> .... had very strong links, through family and religion, to the most important national banks (Banham, 1994: 32).

The Quakers are well known for their charity to the poor and efforts were made by Reverend Temple Chevallier, BD, who resided at the castle, and Backhouse to educate the children of Durham City. Ignatius Bonomi, also a resident of the Bailey, formed a committee to investigate the needs of the City's children. (Cranfield, 1993: 71). J.C. Backhouse speaking in November 1853 said:

> He looked forward to the day when the public mind of
> this country would be roused and disposed to enter on
> the question of Ragged Schools as a national one that
> they should not be allowed to depend on the chance
> contributions of the charitable (Durham Chronicle, 18th.
> November 1853, quoted in Cranfield, ibid: 80).

This shows the philanthropic nature of some of the
leading citizens of Durham City. At the same time,
Cranfield also reminds us of the problem of the
dangerous classes to the capitalist classes (ibid).

5 THE SLUM

As we concentrate on the Irish population regarding the social and economic class and their residence in Durham City, I provide here a brief description of a sample of that population in order to understand their situation.

By the mid-nineteenth century the notion of social groups living intimately together and having common interests was eclipsed (Stein, 1960). As society, both here and abroad, became more fragmented, dissipative, and complex (For an exposition of Complexity Theory see: Harvey, and Reed, 1994,

1996; Prigogine, and Stengers, 1984; Cilliers, 1998; Byrne, 1998). Accordingly, the type of traditional social relations which, when interwoven, comprised 'community', became less relevant at this time (Krannich, and Greide, 1990: 61).

Complex social systems are not simple, they have many components and interactions, not just a few. The historical situation of the immigrant Irish is a complex one. Accordingly, the need to consider the previous complex economic, cultural, and social situation of the immigrant Irish to Durham really matters in his study. Any study of a complex social system that doesn't consider time is not complete - it's like taking a picture of a process without looking at how it got there. It's like thinking about how Anglo-Irish culture influenced a Gaelic community in Ireland without looking at the history behind it. It is important, therefore, to first consider some history of the immigrant Irish to Durham.

The immigrant Irish to Durham City after 1848 were an example of some of the poorest residents in the city. This is clear from their history as a peasant class fleeing from intolerable poverty, disease, and disorder in Ireland during this period. When the census returns of the nineteenth century are consulted it is overwhelmingly clear that the Irish immigrants who came to the Northeast of England were from the Provinces of Connaught and Ulster. Of the estimated 850 Irish-born residents of Durham City in 1851, only 173 stated their county of birth. In descending numerical order, these comprised counties, Mayo (41), Roscommon (29), Dublin (20), Sligo(16), Leitrim (10), Down (8), Monaghan (7), Antrim (7), Galway (6), Armagh (5), Cork (4), Tyrone (3), Louth (3), Limerick (3), Kilkenny (2), Tipperary (1), Londonderry (1), Kings County (1), Kildare (1), Kerry (1), Fermanagh (1), Donegal (1), Clare (1), Cavan (1) (Butler, 1992).

In a limited number of instances, the parish or town in which an individual was born was additionally declared in the enumerator's books. Not one of the above forty-one Mayo-born residents stated a more specific topographical reference to their place of birth than that county. But it is interesting to note that of these forty-one, thirty-three resided in adjacent dwellings in the relatively small neighbourhood of New Elvet, another area associated with poverty.

As both a centre of Catholicism and a visual representation of Anglicanism, the ensuing social mix in Durham City provides an exciting empirical study that clearly lends itself to a complex interpretation. The closed Anglican nature of Durham University up until the 1860's (Heesom, 1992), assumes an anti-Catholic bias and it is known that local Anglicans referred to Durham Catholics as, 'chiefly of low rank, plebeians, common people' (Gooch, 1993:34). As a high percentage of the Catholic population of Durham City were Irish, Anglicans were talking about the Irish.

McDonnell's study of the Irish in Durham City between 1841 and 1861 (McDonnell, 1991) provides us with a good statistical account of this community where the majority of Irish-born were employed in labouring occupations and a few others employed in more skilful work. However, McDonnells' difficulty of accurately establishing the birthplaces of the Irish-born residents of the City using the marriage records of St. Cuthbert's Catholic Church is obvious. The calculations were limited, as only those undergoing a marriage ceremony had the opportunity to state the place of abode of their parents in Ireland, and many did not choose to do so in any case. So, McDonnell's figures, like, indeed, the census data, can only be an estimation of some social statistics. Nevertheless, McDonnell's research does agree with the above census estimates, in that Counties Roscommon and Mayo are the highest of the group of the origin of the Irish-born in Durham City.

McDonnell's research also confirmed what is known from numerous other studies of the place of birth of Irish immigrants to Britain: the greatest numbers came from the Province of Connaught – comprising Counties Mayo, Roscommon, Sligo, Leitrim, and Galway. These counties were in the poorest and most congested western regions of rural Ireland and the inhabitants felt the effects of the famine much worse than elsewhere. In County Mayo, where nearly ninety per cent of the population were dependent on the potato, what is popularly remembered as the Irish Potato Famine, was particularly severe. By 1848, a feeling of total misery and despair already existed in the County Mayo and people were dying and emigrating in their thousands (O'Hara, and Ómuraíle, 2002).

Many harrowing stories of social hardship existed at the time elsewhere in Ireland but in County Mayo conditions were particularly harsh. In the Parish of Ballinrobe, for instance, it was reported that a dead body was washed up on the beach and a starving man eat the heart and liver. Meanwhile, a forlorn young girl carried the corpse of her mother on her back for three miles so that she could make her wants known to the relieving officer - she simply wanted a coffin to bury her parent (The Times, 23.5.1849). In a letter of 1849, addressed to the Prime Minister, Sir Robert Peel, the Protestant rector of the Parish narrated these and other horrifying tales of human misery and asked:

> What, in the name of Heaven, is to become of us? What
> are we to do? The country is gone! We must thus again
> and again strive to arouse you, my Lord, for it is not

possible that you or the English people can be fully conscious or alive to the true state of things in the west of Ireland (ibid).

In neighbouring County Leitrim, a county of 27,192 families, 21,663 (75.3%) were employed in agriculture (1841 Census of County Leitrim) and the sub-division of land within families over the centuries had added to the problem of poverty. By the 1840's, many families' portions of land had decreased to a situation where some were subsisting on little more than a piece of land the size of a conventional garden. In Leitrim, as in the rest of the west of Ireland:

If a man thinks he is near death, and he has six acres and three sons, he will give them two acres apiece and they will do the same: so that the holding is dwindled away to a cabbage garden (The Devon Commission, 1845, Part 1: 605).

In the 1840's townland culture of County Leitrim, labourers worked for a maximum of 10d a day only in harvest periods and were usually unemployed between the months June and August and December and March. Their accommodation and diet were wretched and, 'they would be delighted to emigrate if given the chance' (First Report of the Commissioners, 1836).

Case Studies

Born in the town of Manorhamilton, in County Leitrim, Hugh Sheridan, was to be so 'delighted' to leave Ireland by the end of the 1840's and begin a more promising future as a labourer in Durham City. Living at 24b Silver Street in 1851 Hugh, a thirty-two-year-old labourer now had a wife, twenty-three old Bridget from County Sligo, and a two-month-old son, James, born in Durham (1851 Census of Durham City, Folio 99: 1). Other Irish inhabitants appeared to have better economic prospects than the Sheridans' Their neighbours in Silver Street, the O'Neil's from the eastern seaboard of Ireland, Downpatrick in County Down, were dealers in furniture (1851 Census, Folio 102).

Also, from Manorhamilton, James Gilroy, his son, Thomas, Eleanor Gilroy and her daughters, Mary, and Eleanor, had also left their homes in County Leitrim and settled in the Sherburn Road area of Durham City (Census, Durham City, 1851). Although under the category of 'have-nots', in contrast to the Sheridans, the Gilroys were tradespeople and were likely to be better-off than the Sheridans. Thirty-six-year-old James Gilroy was a master shoemaker, and working alongside him as his apprentice was his thirteen-year-old son Thomas. In a neighbouring house were sixty-seven-year-old Eleanor Gilroy and her daughters, Mary, and Eleanor, employed as milliners. They were likely to have been the mother and sisters of James the shoemaker (1851 Census of Durham City, Folios 184-185).

At 57d Hallgarth Street we find a total of eight Irish-born residents headed by the Killion family and their lodgers. These included John McManus, a twenty-eight-year-old labourer and his twenty-three-year-old wife, Bridget, and their three-month old daughter Ann, born in Durham (1851 Census, Durham City). John and Bridget had married in St. Cuthbert's Roman Catholic Church, Durham City and from church records we learn that Bridget's family were the

Mahon's of Frenchpark, County Roscommon.
Witnesses at the marriage were the Dempseys',
another Roscommon family (ibid). County
Roscommon was traditional grazier county where the
limestone soils were good for pasture, the land was
incomparable in the country and the pastures were
beautiful and fertile (Weld, 1832: 181). Accordingly,
land was at a premium as agrarian capitalism, in the
form of the move from tillage to 'ranching,' rapidly
developed. An intricate system of sub-letting of land
between tenants and landless labourer's families
aggravated this situation. To facilitate development,
the clearance of hundreds of cottiers from the land
was undertaken by many Roscommon landowners to
increase the amount of grazing over tillage. Lord de
Freyne of Frenchpark was the owner of 25,436 acres
in the county and spent long periods away from his
estates. As a powerful absentee landlord, he did not
take an active part in the affairs of his tenants, and the
county.

The consequent hegemonic culture that ensued meant
that the capitalist creativity of landowners, like Lord

de Freyne, continually threatened the status quo of social life. As part of the poorer classes, Bridget Mahon and her family, natives of Frenchpark, would have had direct experience of the deteriorating situation on de Freyn's estates. Roscommon rents, between £7- £10 per acre, were very high and out of financial reach of the landless labouring classes like the Mahon's. Like their neighbours in Durham City, the Furys', also from Frenchpark (1851 Census, Durham City; Marriage Records, St. Cuthbert's Roman Catholic Church, Elvet, Durham City), they may have taken part in the march for food to the gates of de Freyne's Frenchpark mansion prior to leaving Ireland (The Devon Commission, 1845, Witness 448).

At Back Lane, Durham City lived the fifty-three-year-old shoemaker Joseph Tipping born in Manchester and his wife, Ruth who was from Dungannon in County Tyrone, north-eastern Ireland. Also from Tyrone was Edward Donnally, a carpet weaver who was living with his wife Mary, born at Trimdon, Durham ((ibid). Linen weaving was synonymous with

Tyrone and Edward had obviously adapted his skills from linen to carpets.

When we compare the death rates of this social class in Durham City with The Peninsular area, it is evident that deaths rates were lower in the latter. Detail is shown in Figure 8 of a comparison of deaths between Peninsular parishes and other streets in the city with the lowest death rate scaled downwards in the table. The Peninsular Parishes clearly have a reduced, although small, rate of death. The Paving Committee at this time classed sewage facilities as either, Good, Imperfect and None. The reason for a small annual death rate at the College could probably be due to few families residing there, especially with children. Between 1841 and 1851 total deaths in the Peninsular were 101.

Table 8

Seven Lowest Areas of Mortality by Street, 1841-1851

Street	Annual Death Rate per 1000	Total Deaths	Life Expectancy
College	13.7	15	31.0
Allergate	17	28	37.4
Market Place	17.9	56	34
South Bailey	17.9	19	35.4
Millburngate	18.2	32	34.0
Goal	18.6	41	31.3
Church Street	19.8	135	27.2
Old Elvet	20.5	99	39.7
Queen Street	21.0	10	46.8
King Street	21.4	65	26.7
Hallgarth Street	22.2	149	32.0

6 POLICE OF CRIME AND DISORDER

After providing service to the citizens of Durham
City since 1836, the Durham City Borough Police
disbanded in 1921 and amalgamated with Durham
County Constabulary. The remit of the city force had
been to patrol the 330 acres comprising the cathedral
peninsular and Framwellgate – home to over 9000
residents. Then, as it is today, a bastion of religion
and commerce at one end of the social and economic
spectrum and a lack of privilege on the other,
Victorian Durham City strongly reflected an
environmental culture of haves and have nots. And
how seriously police took the duty of applying a
balanced form of justice in this polarized setting is a
question as relevant then as it is today.

Effectiveness and Efficiency

The Durham City Borough Police had been created under the Municipal Corporations Act 1935 to provide a uniformed force to patrol the streets and keep the peace. This was the beginning of a new era for policing, in which an organized and disciplined national force would better cope with spiralling law and order problems spawned by urban capitalism and a rapidly increasing population. By 1870 the force had grown to thirteen officers headed by a superintendent, or high constable, as he was sometimes called. It is interesting to note that at a time when the population of the area had increased massively and contained a great number of non-English-born residents, especially Irish and Scottish, the officers of the force were clearly English to a man.

The complainants were invariably the better-off residents and tradesmen of the city, and the main targets were no different than they are today – working-class young persons. The register reveals years of youthful disorder, nuisance, and delinquency, shattering the myth of a bygone age of peace and tranquillity. But my strongest impression of these complaints lay in the sheer weight of them being made by the middle and upper classes and the absence of complaints from those of the majority population. Out of five hundred or so incidents reported, those made by the lower classes could be counted on one hand. This was truly policing in a hegemonic culture where the bourgeoisie and commercial classes saw the force as a tool to perpetuate bourgeoisie ethos.

Whereas the tax-paying upper classes must have felt the need to get their money's worth from the force, the non-taxpaying poor of Victorian Durham City must have perceived them as unwelcome intrusions into their lives. The frequent references to obstruction of the highway by all kinds of articles and transportation and the need for officers to 'move on' the obstructions, vividly conveys the priority for police to keep the course of capitalism flowing freely in the streets of the city. And the coming of the 'new police' to Durham City clearly signalled a closer monitoring of the patterns of working-class lives. Street gambling, playing musical instruments in the Bailey, swimming in the River Wear on Sundays, running races 'naked' in Houghall Wood and children's games, such as bowling hoops in Framwellgate, are regular entries in the register.

At the end of September 1829, the provision of public safety in Britain ostensibly began to move away from the domain of the 'private' towards the 'public'. As the first detachment of Peel's state-financed Bobbies paraded on the streets of London a new and equitable policing service was heralded, and with it ended an historical era during which the British state had provided little financial support for public safety. This new and unmitigated policing service, based upon state provision through taxes, was further developed outside London after 1835 when the Municipal Corporations Act directed that all boroughs in England and Wales must appoint professional uniformed police officers. It seemed, at last, as if the provision of policing was to become everyone's fate, not just a restricted choice available for the benefit of an elite few. Today, one hundred and ninty-five years on from Peel's policing initiative, it is interesting to note that the provision of policing services is beginning to move back from the 'public' towards the 'private' - to move from fate back to choice once again (McManus, 1995).

Responding expeditiously to the new act of 1835, Durham City soon became a corporation and, under a Watch Committee, appointed five constables to form the Durham City Borough Police on 5th. January 1836. The force existed independently of numerous other local police forces. Encircled by the neighbouring Durham County Constabulary, the city force's remit was to patrol an area of 330 acres and provide unmitigated service to the 9269 residents of the city. The city force continued to remain independent until 1921 when it amalgamated with the Durham County Constabulary (Watson and Harrison, 1990). In the relatively secular-less period in which the Durham City force was established, the apparent peacefulness of the city was being attributed more to the powerful influence of its bishop and the Church of England than to its recently installed police force:

> It is a singular fact that out of more than fifty prisoners tried at our last Assizes but one - and that for an assault merely - had been committed from this city. How will the radicals account for so small an amount of crime in an episcopal city? demoralised by the residence of a Dean, twelve Prebendaries, minor Cannons etc. etc (Durham Advertiser, 16.3.1838.).

By the 1860's, however, this apparent spiritual influence of the church appeared to be weakening as the recorded crime rate soared in Durham City. During the year ending 29th. September 1860, 260 persons were apprehended (21 for indictable offences - 19 went for trial); 289 were summonsed; 549 brought before the Magistrates; 60 prostitutes were charged; 168 persons were charged with drunkenness, 124 males and 44 females, 69 males and 31 females apprehended were discharged with a reprimand from the Bench, it being in nearly every case their first offence. Of the 289 summonses 115 were discharged and 174 convicted (Durham City Police Superintendent's Report, 29.9.1860.). A more realistic and likely alternative explanation for this rise in crime would have been the increase in population and the

then developed organisational effectiveness of the
Durham City Borough Police. But much of the
business of Durham City Borough Police at this time
was concerned with less serious incidents than
attracted the considerations of the Assize or Petty
Sessional Courts. These incidents involved the minor
complaints made by residents of the city, or 'beat
complaints' as they are known to the police. We now
examine the nature and characteristics of the minor
beat complaints made to the Durham City Borough
Police during the period 1860 to 1871.

These complaints were recorded in a single leather-
bound register – the register. The records relating to
these were contained in the original register held in
the force library of Durham Constabulary, Aykley
Heads, Durham City, which had previously come into
my possession. Through analysing these, and other
local police records, I seek to identify how equitably
the force was able to apply its unmitigated remit to
provide a service to all social classes in the city. In a
much wider sense, I attempt to assist in a popular
debate between critical and non-critical scholars of

police history who have argued their positions on exactly who the police of the period were servicing (Critchley, 1978 versus White, 1838). From the critical perspective the position has been cleverly summed up in the following terms:

> Because the English Bourgeois finds himself reproduced in his law, as he does in his God, the policeman's truncheon has for him a wonderful soothing power. But for the workingman quite otherwise (Marx and Engels, 1962: 263).

Accordingly, I hope to make some conclusions about such claims by demonstrating the pattern of freedom and constraint in the life-histories of this small sample, and the dynamic relationship between them and a fragment of the institutional structure of criminal justice around which they lived and worked. To assist in the necessary social class comparisons, again, I have focused particularly on the underprivileged Durham community of the period. It must be recognised, however, that the study is based upon a small geographical area and a limited data source and, therefore, cannot necessarily be seen as representative of other police forces of the period. In addition to the central question of equality of provision, I briefly consider the level of bureaucratic management of officers by this period, the types of minor complaint made and the social identity of offenders.

It could be expected that the minor beat complaint register, examined here, would represent a realistic picture of a fragment of the social life of the greater part of the population of Durham City - for whilst most residents of the city would not have found themselves involved in incidents of the more serious criminal kind, it is likely they would have regularly experienced the less serious matters traditionally subject of police minor beat complaints. Such complains often resulted from annoyance caused by neighbours and children or disorderly revellers passing through the neighbourhood.

The beat complaint recording procedure in the 1860's was much the same as it is today. A police officer received a complaint from a member of the public, the officer recorded the complaint in a register, it was subsequently read by other constables as they came on duty, and as they patrolled their beats they were expected to watch out for the nuisance and take appropriate action to prevent recurrences of the complaint. The following section considers the personnel of the force - the watchers - during the period in question and how bureaucracy and discipline impacted upon their daily lives.

The Watchers

Some of the earliest records of Durham City Police - the watchers - can be found in The Durham Directory, 1854 and 1857. Superintendent William Robison is Head Constable. He is also recorded as the Billet Master for the Corporation of Durham. At this early time, we can see from the Borough of Durham Reports of Inspectors of Constabulary (DCRO/Du 1/59) that the approximate population of the city was 13,743, the area of the city was 8,599 acres, the number of constables was 13 and that the ratio of population to an individual constable was 1057.

The police force at that time consisted of one Superintendent, two Sergeants, and 10 Constables. According to the Inspectors, when inspected it was seen to be complete in number and presented the appearance of a well-chosen and respectable body of men, remarkably well clothed and well supplied with the requisite accoutrements, all of which were in good serviceable condition. The charge - room, though small, and not very spacious, and the cells for prisoners, notwithstanding their being open to objection for reasons assigned in former reports, were reasonably clean and in good order. In addition to his ordinary duties, the Superintendent discharges those of Billet Master, Inspector of weights and measures, and Inspector of common lodgings. The Sergeants were Inspectors of nuisances, and the Constable on duty at the police office acted as assistant relieving officer from 4 to 9 p.m. In the opinion of the Inspector, the force had been maintained in a satisfactory state of discipline and efficiency.

William Robison, married Jane Scott on 28 Nov 1840 at the Parish Church of Chester-le-Street in the

County of Durham, occupation Policeman, residence Market Place Durham, his father being William Robison, Countryman. As the city police station was in the Market Place, it would seem that Robison was already a constable in the city force at this earlier time. The 1851 Census of Durham, Civil Parish of St Nicholas, records Superintendent Robison residing at 51 Claypath. Durham Directory has him at 50 Claypath.

The Census shows William Robison, born 1815 Burnfoot, Northumberland, England Superintendent of Police. His wife, Jane, was born 1823 Netherslaw, Northumberland, England. They had two children, Mary Ann Robison, born 1844 St Nicholas, Durham, England, and William Robison, born 1850 St Nicholas, Durham, England.

Little more is known of Robison or his men but from the Durham Advertiser dated 14th July 1854 we find a letter was printed from Superintendent Robison of Durham Police criticising the Durham Coroner who had criticised PC's Beuglass and Drysden in the investigation of the death of John Farrow who had drowned in the River Wear. Two men had been taken into custody following the drowning and were released from police custody after investigation. The coroner had complained that the prisoners should have been taken before the magistrate for his decision before being released. Superintendent Robison reproached the coroner for interfering in a police investigation.

According to the Inspectors of Police, it would seem that the city force was sufficiently effective and efficient and that a new administration was not needed at this time, yet changes were afoot.

Figure 4. William Robison (centre) Superintendent of Police Durham City 1848-57 (Public Domain).

Superintendent Robison had left the force in 1857. Police Constable William Beuglass, mentioned earlier, also left the force in 1857 and transferred as Sergeant to Northumberland Police (British Police History online, https://british-police-history.uk/f/durham-city accessed 10.12.2003). PC Beuglass is shown in the following image with a group of Durham City officers, who appear to be dressed in a more modern design of uniform (ibid).

Figure 5. Durham City Police Officers about 1850. PC William Beuglass is standing second on the left (Public Domain).

It is only a few years later that we see some personnel changes. Between 1861 and 1868 the personnel of the

Durham City force fluctuated between nine and thirteen officers. During this time some officers left the force and others joined. William Beard, born in Tintwistle, Cheshire in 1830, was the Superintendent and High Constable for the borough. He resided at 4, Western Hill and later in Allergate. The Sergeants were Robert Ruddick of Magdalen Street, Richard Clarkson of New Elvet and William Webster of Sherburn Road (Walker's Durham Directory and Almanack, 1861-1868: 8; 87: 10).

At this time the Police Station was part of the Town Hall situated at 27, Market Place but in later years was re-located to Claypath. Police uniform and accoutrements were provided by the Watch Committee, who also fixed rates of pay and ranks. A Merit Class Sergeant, promoted by the Watch Committee for meritorious conduct and general efficiency, was paid thirty-three shillings and sixpence per week while a Merit Class Constable was paid twenty-seven shillings and sixpence (Durham City Borough Police, Superintendent's Annual Report 31.5.1876).

The strength of the city police in September 1860 had been reduced from earlier to ten; one Superintendent, two Sergeants and seven Constables. Three officers had been reported for misconduct in the previous twelve months - one of which had been discharged and the other two reprimanded. Speaking of the officers at this time, Superintendent Beard had said:

> .....for the last six months during which I have had command of the force I have found them all very attentive to their duties (Durham City Borough Police, Superintendent's Annual Report 29.9.1860.).

They certainly would have needed to be attentive, for in the small borough area they policed during that period there were ninety-nine public houses and five beer houses. Fourteen of the former and one of latter licence holders were summonsed for offences against the licence in the twelve-month period to September 1860. There were twenty-four common lodging houses, all of which had been well conducted, none having been summonsed for breaches of the Common Lodging House Act within the previous twelve months in question. In the same twelve-month period fifty-nine robberies were reported to the

police, the value of property stolen amounting to
£180 7s 6d of which £90 9s 6d in value was
recovered; seventy-six premises were found insecure
by the police and there were thirty-seven cattle found
straying in the streets (ibid).

Public concern during this period for effective social
control poses the question about the level of progress
made towards a more bureaucratic and efficient
policing structure for the force. The register of minor
complaints (the register) is helpful here as the General
Orders of the force had been entered in it. These
orders comprise operational instructions and general
information from the superintendent to the men on
the ground to how they should go about their duties.

As a disciplined force, but where individual discretion
of officers was also an organizational expectation,
there was a need for Superintendent Beard to show a
forceful management style to maintain discipline. It is
easy for the reader of the register to interpret the
tenor of some of his instructions as conveying an

atmosphere of disagreement and disharmony between him and the officers he managed. As the following entry in the register demonstrates, there was a constant need to remind the men of their duty and instil in them a sense of loyalty and service:

> 30th. May,1864. In consequence of PC 9 Isaac Brown having resigned his situation through a mistaken idea that he ought to have been on duty at Mr. Wharton's Park on the 7th. Inst. in place of some other officer, the Superintendent, for the information of the men and Sergeants will in future place such men on special duty where extra pay will be given as best does their duty on other occasions. This, it is to be hoped, will have a tendency to put a stop to several of the officers who continually pass three-quarters of their time in talking when on duty.........It is quite clear that PC Isaac Brown did not come here with the intention of staying but should he, or any of the other men, think to better themselves by coming here and going into any other Police Force they will make a very big mistake indeed. Should anyone dislike the nature of Police Duties and intend leaving it will be better for themselves and everybody else if they would do so. Signed: William Beard, Superintendent.

This order soon came back to haunt Superintendent Beard for, in such a position of authority and example-setting, he was himself open to observation and criticism if he transcended the rules and expectations of his men, as the following entry illustrates:

> 23rd. November 1864. Robert Ruddick having been discharged from this force for insubordination to the Superintendent and other misconduct and it having been reported to the Superintendent that he had for a long time past been tampering with the men in many ways such as 'have you seen the Superintendent, was he drunk' and in many other similar ways including, 'I am keeping a book against that gentleman let me know everything you see I will put him right some day. I will let him see who is the master here' and such other childish nonsense, the Superintendent expects that from this date to prevent any of the men being so foolishly led astray, the Sergeant will pay every attention to matters of this nature in order that the men may not lead themselves into trouble. Signed: William Beard, Superintendent.

As well as some disapproval from within the force, members of the public also complained about the behaviour of officers. Like other areas of Britain, complaints against the police in Durham City were very often from the upper classes (Critchley, 1978). One feasible reason for this was the higher rates the upper classes had to pay to maintain the local police. This inevitably lead to certain members of the community taking a close interest in whether the police were providing value for money. Some close public scrutiny of the Durham City officers did take place and several complaints were recorded from the more influential residents of the city:

> 16th. April 1864. Mr. Wharton, Dryburn, complains that the Durham Police are a set of careless inefficient men who when passing through the street he frequently sees children riding behind carriages, coals laying in the streets and other nuisances annoying to passengers and the Police taking no notice of them whatever. Signed: Richard Clarkson, Sergeant.

The traditional principle of police 'giving way' to others when on the footpath reflected the servile attitude the public expected from the police officer. But this was not always practised by Durham City Officers and complaints were received to this effect. Some complaints of officer's behaviour were quite serious and, if not reflections of professional incompetence, they must have surely bordered on criminal conduct.

> 18th. April 1864. In consequence of a statement having been made before the Magistrates this morning by Catherine Gilbertson that when brought to the Police Station last night P.C. 10 attempted to search her by feeling to her bosom and putting his hand to her underclothing, the Superintendent for the guidance of the Force Generally Orders that from this date no officer will attempt to search any female under any circumstances whatever. Signed: William Beard, Superintendent.

As crucial elements of capitalism, bureaucracy and order are likely to be unnatural elements of human relations management. Accordingly, bureaucracy and order provoked an obvious conflict between the managers and those they managed. This can be identified in the tone of the entries in the register and the sheer routine nature of police-work and bureaucratic administration expressed in the text. The bureaucratic organisation of police-work demonstrated in the pages of the register represents the most rational form of administration. It was methodical and predictable and produced a form of organisation based upon practical means-ends calculations and expertise in police-work. As part of the overall capitalist order, the police organisation was responding to the inherent need for bureaucracy as any other institution of the time, commercial or otherwise, would have done. Efficient organisation was necessary to ensure the effective eradication of the nuisance being reported. An important need here was for officers to identify the persons responsible. The primary category of offender is considered in the next section.

The Watched

The notion that a bygone age of public tranquillity
existed on the streets of Britain has been a popular
issue of discussion for generations. Children, as a
major cause of minor street nuisance is also a
recurring theme in social history yet, in contrast to the
coming of the period of the 'new' police, many
commentators looked back affectionately upon an
apparent age of youthful honour and respect towards
the law and parental authority:

> From this relaxation of parental discipline……..doth
> come to pass that children who have been brought up
> within these thirty years, have nothing like the same
> reverence and submission to their parents…....This is
> the cause of juvenile depredation: this is the chief cause
> of the increase of crime, especially amongst
> children……….Oh, oh! what a burden hath the Lord laid
> upon his ministers, to stand amidst the wreck of a
> dissolving society, and like Canute, to preach unto the
> surging waves (Irving, 1829).

In contrast to 'the good old days' before the 'new'
police, it was also claimed that the years following
their inception were thick with juvenile delinquency
and disorder. Such comparative analyses today also
result in conclusions that contemporary crime levels
in Britain are dangerously high and in need of tough

responses by the police and the courts - 'short sharp shock treatment'. The notion that law and order is hopelessly out of control in comparison to past times is seriously challenged by some writers who have shown that the seriousness and incidence of crime in past centuries is no different from today. For instance, it has been claimed that 'a twenty-year rule' exists which has been constantly used by the politically and economically powerful who assert that life was so much more tranquil and idyllic twenty years earlier, when in fact, nothing much changes (Pearson, 1983).

The data available from the register tends to support part of the latter theory in that, in relation to the activity of children's behaviour on the streets today, nothing has really changed from the 1860's. During this period in Durham City the primary culprits of minor complaints made by residents to the police were children. The categories and numbers of persons recorded in the register as responsible for incidents reported to the police were 94 boys, 41 children, 8 young men, 3 girls, 19 men, 1 prostitute, 1 police officer and 132 unidentified persons. In incorporating the categories of 'boys' and 'girls' with 'children', it becomes quite clear that 'children' were the largest group of offenders:

> 14th. June, 1864 The Recorder complains of the way great annoyance is caused in Framwellgate by children shouting and brawling in the street, bowling hoops, playing at ball against the houses, marking the front of the houses with chalk and other unpleasant matters, and requests that the Police when in that direction will pay a little more attention to the By-laws relating to the above mentioned complaint................... Signed: William Beard, Superintendent.

Statements on the need for discipline and order for children in the early nineteenth century were common in publications and in the written objectives of reformatory and industrial schools where poor children attended - like the Ragged Schools. Such schools taught the need to form principles of conduct as a basis for the formation of useful habits - which included the habit of industry. A primary objective of these schools was to free the poor and the state from parish relief and to inculcate values of labour, independence, and society. Like many other cities, Durham had its Ragged School which was situated at Clock Mill, Millburngate and whose objectives were:

> To relieve the public from juvenile vagrancy, mendicancy, and consequent depravity. To rescue as many children from degradation and misery. To prepare them for a useful and respectable course of life. To try the power of kindness over the young and destitute. Thus, to discharge a Christian duty towards a class which particularly requires attention and amelioration (Walker's Durham Directory and Almanac, 1861 :8).

Whilst not missing the crucial welfare aspects of attending to such children, it is important to note a tendency on behalf of part of Victorian upper-class society to act as moral entrepreneurs and crusaders in such matters. The good working-class family unit, supportive of industrial society, was assured through such moral crusades (Ignatieff, 1981: 37-59).

The Nuisance

From a critical perspective the new administration of the police system was designed principally to deal with a working-class culture wherein particular targets of offence were invariably to be found. The primary targets of public concern were serious crime, political unrest, industrial strikes, the eradication of irregular economies and the eradication of traditional street

cultures such as gambling, ballgames, and other
working-class leisure pursuits (Mayhew, 1981:160-
172). Examples of crime and the policing of
traditional street cultures can be found in the register,
however, there is an absence of incidents relating to
industrial disputes and political unrest. Working-class
leisure pursuits were also monitored by the police:

> 15th. March 1862. Superintendent Beard received
> information from Mr William Linsey of New Elvet that
> every Sunday about 2pm there is a number of young men
> assemble in the first field to the right hand through the
> Archway in Framwellgate for the purpose of playing
> pitch and toss and Mr. Linsey particularly desires that the
> Police will endeavour to put a stop to the nuisance.
> Signed: William Beard, Superintendent.

And further

> 20th. October 1862. Superintendent Beard has received a
> complaint this morning from Mr. Green, Governor of
> the County Prison that every Sunday between the hours
> of 12 am and 2 pm a number of young men assemble in
> Maiden Castle Woods for the purpose of running foot
> races naked................ Signed: Richard Clarkson,
> Sergeant.

In the period between 1860 and 1871 the register
shows the primary categories of minor complaint to
be 48 instances of damage, 33 of brawling, 27 of
shouting, 20 of throwing stones, 12 of knocking on

doors and ringing door bells, 9 of gambling, 5 of noise, 4 of bathing in the river and 3 of running races.

Damage to property was by far the most reported complaint, complainants being most usually property owners of some financial substance. The second most reported complaint was brawling, which offence in most cases merely amounted to young persons raising their voices in the streets. Some evidence exists to support the view that the police in Durham City in the 1860's were involved in restricting the traditional street culture and working-class leisure pursuits. In addition to complaints of running races and gambling in public places mentioned earlier, there were several complaints of people bathing in the River Wear and playing musical instruments in the streets.

The next section looks at the primary category of complainant of street nuisance. More than any other data in the register, identification of this category is likely to assist in answering the principle question raised in this study; to what extent were the police providing unmitigated equality of provision to the inhabitants of Durham City?

The Complainants

At the inception of the new police in 1829 many of the better off members of society objected to contributing higher taxes to the upkeep of the police while the less well-off suspected the primary police function was to watch and monitor them as a 'dangerous class' (Radzinowicz, 1968). The true identification of the primary recipients of policing provision is at the centre of an intellectual argument polarised between Classicist and Marxist writers.

Classicism with its emphasis on private property, assumes that all citizens are free, rational, and equal, no one citizen having priority of rank or status in the eyes of the law (Young, 1981: 253-26) while, from a Marxist perspective, partiality of justice favours the economically privileged. According to the Classicist view of police history, the poor and property-less inhabitants of Durham City had as much to gain from the introduction of the 'new' police as the upper classes (Critchley, 1978: 24-8). In contrast, however, the new police of Durham City would have been an intimidating and oppressive tool of the capitalist state (White, ibid: 58-9).

As a result of the Municipal Corporations Act, the reform of rural policing in the Durham area was well advanced by the early 1860's and, according to the Classicist view, it could be expected that the larger proportion of the local population were benefiting from the new institutional structure of public policing provision. The total population of Durham City at that time was 14088 and consisted of 12720 English-born, 898 Irish-born, 398 Scottish-born and 72 others, the greater proportion of which were not privileged classes (Census of England and Wales, 1861, Durham City). The Irish population of Durham City is, again, a useful lower-class group to consider as potential complainants to the police.

As a settled community, the Irish were relatively new in Durham, most having fled from famine in the previous decade and a half. As a consequence, they were suffering the natural effects of that situation which impacts upon first-generation immigrants - poverty, low wages, and employment status. The perception of the Irish by the host community is likely, as earlier seen, to have been influenced by the local press, which appeared to have an unkind obsession with the Irish, their religion, and their appearance (McManus, 1989). The following from a newspaper article was not uncommon:

> We cannot believe that any class of men, or any peculiar(sic) people can be so constituted to rejoice at living in an element of dirt, filth, and wretchedness on the one hand, or always living in a constant turmoil on the other; in an interminable interchange of hostilities with those around them. Yet this seems to be the character of the Irish (Durham Advertiser, 8.1.1836.).

In 1861 the highest populated area of Irish-born in Durham City was in the low-rented, slum-tenement area of Framwellgate where 14.6% of the total Irish-born of the City were resident (Census of England and Wales, 1861, Durham City). That the Framwellgate area was classified a health hazard reflected well the poverty-stricken condition of its residents. The state of health in the City had been examined in the 1850's and findings showed that the two highest areas of Irish residence, Framwellgate and Water Lane in Elvet, were the unhealthiest areas of the City with the highest death rate (Doctor Oliver's Report on Durham, 1852/3/4/ DCRO, Ref. Du/3/13).

By 1861 the Durham City Irish were well settled and employed as general labourers (27%), agricultural labourers (21%); factory workers (2.7%); hawkers (6.6%); servants (3.5%); coalminers (11.3%); navies (6.7%); other, (21.2%), including fiddler, bagpipe maker, astronomer, soldier and 'compulsory visitor to the police station' (Census of England and Wales, 1861, Durham City). The largest populated parishes, Framwellgate (4326) and Elvet (4140) (Whellan, 1894: 40-41) were still the popular Irish domiciles. Areas such as Framwellgate were the places where many of the better-off believed criminals congregated and by the1840's it had become a fundamental principle in police-work that you guard one area by watching another. The presence of disease in these areas of bad reputation would also have helped the popular misbelief of the time that disease and crime were coterminous (Alison, 1840: 76).

In view of the need for an active police presence to deal with the perceived problems of social order that Irish immigration brought to Durham, it may not be surprising to find there was concern amongst the Irish population themselves for police over-zealousness towards fellow countrymen. Although the police were vigilant concerning the Irish community harassment on a large scale did not occur, however, individual cases of abuse of authority could obviously be found. The following letter, to the Editor of the Durham Chronicle and headed, 'A Voice From Thornley,' was published on 13th. January 1871 and while being very eloquent and amusing, demonstrates the serious concern some local Irish had about police abuse of power:

> Sir, You would greatly oblige a number of us here in Thornley, if you could find space in your valuable paper for 'A voice from Thornley'. Thornley! where's Thornley? perhaps you will say. Well Sir, it might be in Patagonia, or in the Sandwich Islands; but it isn't, it's in

the County Palatine of Durham. Why on earth, you may ask, do I volunteer this very important topographical information? I'll tell you Mr. Editor because I want to introduce you to an anomaly. Here's the anomaly, come forward my lad, make your bow, and say your say. Anomaly (speaks) - I'm a Thornley policeman, I'm the dread majesty of the law. (Sings) - I'm monarch of all I survey, my right there is none to dispute. (Speaks) Now men and women of Thornley, this is the first and last commandment, I'm the only law in Thornley, thou shalt have no other law but me. Tremble, and move on. (Whack! whack! whack!!!). To be serious, it may be a hideous nightmare, but it seems to me that in Thornley we're entirely out of the pale of the law, that justice, trial by jury, habeas corpus, divorce court, anything, everything, is represented here solely by 'the policeman'. Well may Dame Justice be depicted as blindfold, for poor Paddy from Thornley knows to his cost, that when a pitman is put in one of her scales, and a policeman in the other, the pitman is pretty sure to kick the beam..................I hope, Mr. Editor, that I shall be excused if I see in the justice so liberally dealt out (if not in quality, at least in quantity) to poor Thornley, a most extraordinary and puzzling anomaly. Signed: John McCloskey, Hartlepool Street, Thornley (Durham Chronicle, 13.1.1871).

Identifying the social classes of those who made complaints to the Durham City Police was a simple matter of referring to the area of the text in the register where occupation, or status, and address had been written. In ninety-five per cent of the cases complained of these details had been clearly recorded. To simplify the presentation of the data concerning the variously named occupations or status' I placed each individual reference into thirteen general categories of the 204 complaints made where occupation or status was recorded. These were businessmen (65); lawyers (27); titled persons (19); councillors (15); clergymen (14); doctors (13); landowners (11); mayors (10); academics (9); tradesman (8); military officers (7); prison governors (4) and managers (2). The absence here of working-class occupations is remarkable. No 'labourers', 'miners' or similar occupations were recorded at all. One would assume from this that the lower-class residents of Durham City were existing in a state of entire peace and tranquillity.

In contrast to the register of complaints and complainants made, the register of charges made against individuals tells a quite different story (Charge Book of the Durham City Borough Police, 9.5.1863. DCRO, Ref., Du1/59/8). Between 23.8.1863. and 23.8.1864 656 persons were charged, the majority of whom were listed monotonously as labourers, miners, prostitutes, and other similar occupations. Of 260 persons apprehended during 1860, 3 were of superior education, 3 could read and write well, 118 could read and write, 6 could read only and 130 could neither read nor write (Durham City Borough Police, Superintendent's Annual Report to the Watch Committee for year ending 29.9.1860. DCRO, Ref., Du1/59/233).

There is a sense in which the meaning of the words of Marx and Engels can be reversed to allow in a perception of the existence of a 'soothing power' of contentment amongst those who did not complain - the working-classes (Marx and Engels, 1962: 263). In contrast, the adverse effect of street nuisance on businesspersons in the city is reflected in the high ratio of them who complained to the police. The interference of residents going about their daily business was a common source of complaint from better-off residents of the city, in particular offences of obstructing the highway:

> 22nd. August 1864. Mr. Robson, Cabinet maker and Upholster, Old Elvet, complains that every day between the hours of 12 and 1pm considerable annoyance is caused by a number of men standing in front of his shop smoking and spitting upon the footpath and obstructing the footpath. He desires that the Police will endeavour

to put a stop to this nuisance. Signed: Richard Clarkson, Sergeant.

This type of offence, which must have had some negative impact upon customers and discouraged them from visiting shops, was obviously very annoying to shop owners. The strict policing of footpath nuisance and obstruction could be interpreted as part of the overall police strategy for the free passage of capitalism in the city. There was, however, some evidence of police failure to carefully enforce the rules relating to obstruction and protection of property and such instances were recorded in the register.

Further evidence of the higher social status of complainants is again evident in the location of complainant's addresses. Old Elvet (27); Framwellgate (22); Claypath (16); Church Street (13); Gilesgate(12); New Elvet (12); North Road (10); Saddler Street (10); Market Place (9); South Street (9); Hallgarth Street (8); Elvet Bridge (8); Crossgate (7); Palace Green (7); Silver Street (6); Kepier (5); Sidegate (5); Unknown (62). It is clear from the 1861 Census that Old Elvet was an area where residents were generally of a higher social status and the few working-class residents of the street were usually servants in the richer households. In contrast, the inhabitants of neighbouring Water Lane and Court Lane in 1861 were of a lower economic status to those in Old Elvet. Similarly, Framwellgate's tenement slums were usually rented to the poorer classes through landlords and agents such as John Bramwell, Solicitor of North Bailey. Of the 22 complaints concerning the Framwellgate area several of the complainants, like Mr. Bramwell, who resided elsewhere than Framwellgate, had concerns relating to that area. Of the 22 complaints relating to Framwellgate, complainant's occupations were recorded as: mayor (1); landowner (3); doctor (3); lawyer (6); businessman (7); carter (1); unknown (2).

In this section, the critical perspective on the early police appears to be supported by the contents of the register. The poorer classes of Durham City may well have seen themselves merely as subjects of police surveillance rather than complainants and, contrary to what has been claimed by some writers, like Critchley (op. cit.), there seems little evidence in the register that the poor and property-less of Durham City benefited from the formation of their new police. This is supported by reports of others living closer to the period (White, op. cit.). This may not be surprising, for crime and disorder has always threatened communities and households which are better-off in material terms, and the early institutional foundations of the state were organized around the surveillance and regulation of those 'dangerous' classes who presented that threat.

7 POLICE OF PUBLIC UTILITES

The standard of health and hygiene in Durham City in the early part of the nineteenth century could only be described as wretched. In 1841 the Health of Towns Association drew up a table from official documents in which the city, at 32.2 in every thousand of the population, was shown to have the highest mortality rate in County Durham (Clark, 1849: 8). It was not until 1848, and the introduction of the Public Health Act of that year, that the causes of such high mortality were officially enquired upon. In such a pious and sacred city, where many showed strong belief in, and reverence for, a deity worshipped as having the power over life and death, delaying action until 1848 may well have reflected the idea that God's will would be

114

done - eventually. However, the enquiry report was keen to put into the minds of its readers the *true* perspective of its social ills, as opposed to the aesthetic effect of its skyline and paramount associations with the Christian Church:

> This city is associated in men's minds only with architectural splendour and ecclesiastical dignity; and few persons beyond the bounds of the county are aware of the contrast between that Durham which strangers visit to admire, and that Durham in which 10,000 human beings pass an existence demonstrably shortened by one seventh part (Clark 1849: 28).

Thus, Pasquino's conceptual, 'cluster of practices' in relation to a project involving the improvement of environmental health and safety, was ripe for development in Durham City. However, although the moral training of the population was the primary objective of this health and hygiene project, the focus of moral training had a more specific target – the poor. Procacci (1991) argues that the amoral, pre-industrial commonalities of the poor were seen as the purest form of social danger to the state. And in early nineteenth century industrial Britain this fear still existed. As well as riot and sedition, the state feared the possibility of an anti-society - a zone of

unchecked instinct incompatible with the free
circulation of labour and capital. Furthermore, bad
sanitary practices were the cause of illness and
subsequent loss of labour-power for the bourgeoisie.
Nationally, the cost of sickness and death to the
wealth of the nation was a great worry for bourgeois
society. Lord Morpeth's economic perception of
sickness was typical of his class:

> There are items of expense which may be reckoned to
> be incurred under the present system: direct attendance
> on the sick; loss of what they would have earned;
> premature death of productive contributors to the
> national wealth and expenses of premature funerals
> (Quoted in the Annual Report of the Medical Officer of
> Health for Durham City, 1851-52: 25. DCRO Du
> 3/13/1-2.).

At an earlier moment, in relation to death on the
battlefield, William Petty had declared that each
young Englishman who died represented a net loss to
the state of nineteen pounds sterling (Roncati, 1985).

Cleaning up the Poor

Reporting on the causes of ill health in Durham City
in 1853, some Medical Officers were clear that the
real threat emanated from the poor. Through

instruction, however, it was believed their insanitary culture could be improved:

> There can be little doubt that, by an improved educa-
> tion - the melioration of the social condition of the poor
> - the direct influence of individuals in better and more
> enlightened circumstances - an incalculable good might
> be affected in the poorer classes of society. In those
> abodes of filth, improvidence, and intemperance, there
> dwell persons who struggle so little against that which
> surrounds them, that they become callous to its
> existence, and acclimated to its continuance. There are
> many to whom personal cleanliness is unknown, and by
> whom the decencies and proprieties of social relations
> are unheeded. By this neglect of their domestic
> condition and economy, can it be a matter of surprise
> that they become habituated to the uttermost depths of
> physical degradation and depravity. (Annual Report of
> the Medical Officer of Health for Durham City for the
> year ending 31st. March 1853. DCRO Du 3/13/3.).

It would be necessary, therefore, for the state to create 'the social citizen' of Durham City. The 'science of police' becomes the political device that would defeat recalcitrance amongst the poorer classes and create this improved citizen. Clearly then, the object of The State in nineteenth century Durham City was to produce the inhabitants of the slum as functioning, maximized citizens through better health and hygiene. The development of a stronger, healthier, more hygienic, and morally based working class would be more fitting to capitalist expansion in Durham City. Table 9 shows primary targets topographically available for development.

Table 9

Seven Highest Areas of Mortality by Street, 1841-1851

Street	Annual Death Rate per 1000	Total Deaths	Life Expectancy
Infirmary	251.0	61	35.3
Workhouse	231.5	200	39.9
Dun Cow Lane	58.8	18	39.4
Court Lane	33.7	58	29.3
Leazes Place	31.0	19	19.6
Framwellgate	27.0	369	24.3
South Street	26.8	118	29.9
Crossgate	25.7	157	29.2
Silver Street	25.1	98	27.1
Gilesgate	24.8	415	27.8

(Shaw, 1868).

After the Infirmary, with a death rate of 251.0 per thousand inhabitants, Dun Cow Lane followed with an annual death rate with 58.8 per thousand. Although Gilesgate, in the east, had the highest mortality rate, it is clear from various reports that another of the primary areas of 'social danger', adjacent to the putrid River Wear and regularly referred to by the Medical Officer, existed in the Western Division of the city - the Borough of Framwellgate, whose,

> .... five main streets radiate from its bridge. South Street, running southwards up the river; Milburngate and Framwellgate running northwards, at some little distance down the river; and Crossgate, Allergate and the New North Road, lying between them. Two small brooks, St. Margaret's Beck, and the Clock-Mill Beck, descend on each side of Crossgate and reach the river above and below the bridge (Clark, 1849: 5).

The eastward flow of the River Wear would have taken the sewerage from higher places, such as the Peninsular, to gather in the wear at Framwellgate. The courts and yards of the poorer areas like Framwelgate were already putrid with their own sewerage:

The fact indeed is, that the Commissioners have no control over those courts and yards about which the poor are congregated, and the condition of which is of far more importance to the City and should receive a far larger share of the attention of the ruling body, than the thoroughfares and main streets chiefly inhabited by the rich. These can afford singly to cleanse their own dwellings, an advantage which the poor man can only obtain by a measure of combination (ibid:7).

In 1849, Dr. Watkin, an experienced medical practitioner, stated that epidemic sickness was constantly present in Framwellgate, which was notorious for its low-class lodging-houses (Clark, ibid:9). A later report put the cause of such high mortality as:

............vicious habits, indiscretion, an indolent, or too laborious life, poverty, atmospherical vicissitudes, innutritious, or unwholesome food, and not among the least, imprudent marriages, tending to perpetuate certain kinds of disease beyond the control and jurisdiction of any Board of Health. (Annual Report of Durham City Board of Health for the year ending 31st. March 1853. DCRO Du 3/13/1-2).

Page: 120

In contrast, Doctor Clarke was later to put Framwellgate's problems down to bad water and drainage while Doctor Watkin's analysis surely describes a class identifiable with pauperism defined by:

> .....that kind of indigence which becomes by its extension and intensity a sort of scourge, a permanent nuisance to society (Cherbuliez, 1826: 205).

Surveillance

The Irish inhabitants of Durham City were clearly high on the list of Doctor Watkin's irritants. Although the Irish were present in all the slum areas of the city, in 1848 Doctor Oliver had particularly described the problems of Framwellgate and, taking a class-view of the problem like Doctor Watkin, had recognized the Irish working-class as part of a blameworthy target for unsanitary practices and immorality:

> In some of the houses, five and six beds are contained in a single room; and during the more stirring periods of the year, as at fairs, races, and in harvest, when the town is inundated with Irish labourers, shakedowns, mats, and straw, in addition, are spread on the floor, to afford increased accommodation to the vast influx of vagrants and wayfarers, as it appears to be the invariable practice of the proprietors to cram as many beds into a room as possible. They are excessively crowded, frequently five and six individuals lie in one bed, men women and children indiscriminately, marking the depraved and blunted state of their moral faculties, and the social demoralization which prevails (Oliver, 1848: 20).

121

Here we have a description of pauperism - poverty intensified at the level of *social danger* - as, 'mobility' and 'promiscuity', 'independence', 'ignorance' and 'insubordination' (Procacci, 1991), which required surveillance. Indeed, in 1853, the Officer of Health was prepared to involve the uniformed police in the prevention and detection of these depravities by, 'a systematic and sustained surveillance' (Annual Report of Durham City Board of Health for the year ending 31st. March 1853, DCRO Du 3/13/1-2).

Surveillance, thus, became part of the technique in the fight against *social danger* as the state placed its emphasis on the rules for public hygiene in cities such as Durham. A 'cluster of practices' had developed - the policing of dwellings, rules of hygiene in the workplace, hygiene in marriage and procreation (of Malthusian fame). Hygiene for the state thus exists as:

> …..a grid for reading social relations, a system which serves at once to canalize them (the poor) and to invent new paths of circulation that are more 'orderly' and more decipherable (Procacci, 1991).

Thus, if we accept this view of surveillance of the poor, the health and hygiene project was linked to the process of growth and the establishment of bourgeois control (Foucault, op. cit.). It served the purposes of the medical bourgeois, Drs. Oliver and Watkin, to clarify the identity of the threat. And the Irish were high on the list. Yet, there is nothing, other than Durham City poverty, to categorize the Irish as unhygienic. Indeed, the way of life in rural Ireland, from which the Irish inhabitants of Durham City had fled after 1848, may well have provided far improved environmental hygiene than that of their new-found order in the beautiful City of Durham. One way of conceiving this irony is to briefly consider the important historic similarity between disparate areas of rural Ireland in the period prior to emigration in 1848.

That most Irish immigrants to Durham had moved from pre-famine organized and settled rural pre-industrialization to urban industrialization and social disorganization is clear enough. (For illustrations of historical change from rural to urban societies see

Tonnies, 1957; Redfield, 1947:293-308, Redfield, 1968). Yet, the nature of the community setting in Ireland, and how this impacted upon a way of life, fitted a relatively strong and healthy population. E.P. Thompson's depiction of the Irish as physically more powerful and energetic, in contrast to other non-Irish manual workers of the time, shows quite well the advantages on their health of the pre-industrial labour rhythms they were accustomed to in Ireland (Thompson,1968: 473-5.).

The Townland

Importantly, settled organization for the pre-industrial Irish is exemplified in the Irish land unit known as the 'townland' - a small rural division of the parish of about 350 acres (Connell, Cronin and O' Dalaigh, 1998). As a principal aspect of Irish community life of the time, people identified socially with this land-unit more than any other.

Townland family associations had lasted for centuries and represented a kind of cultural regularity which included a form of sanitary provision which was, in contrast to Durham City, effectively both safe and economical. In the Irish townland farming community absolutely all domestic waste was ploughed back into the soil and broken down through natural biological processes. And the myth of the Irish as unhygienic is revealed by the relative natural and open sanitary conditions of the townland way of life. However, for critics of Irish hygiene, like Doctor Oliver, these alternative genealogical descriptions of Irish origins and functions would rather remain hidden (Kendall and Wickham, 1999:29). What is important to note is the organized social setting of nineteenth century life these people had left behind in Ireland for the urban squalor of cities like Durham. Indeed, in contrast to the dwellings they had left behind those Irish who settled in Durham City found their new homes to be, in their own words,

> .....close, confined, crowded and ill-ventilated (Reid. 1845: 559).

Thus, although descriptions of Irish rural life of the time do not portray excellence in domestic hygiene and health, the picture was one of comparative order and health to the crowded confinement and unhygienic disorder of an English city like Durham. Hence, the cultural characteristics of Durham City were being driven not just ecclesiastically - religious revolution had already had its day in Durham. It was time for another drastic and far-reaching change in ways of thinking and behaving in which the battle against the devil made way for the battle against filth and disease - a health and hygiene project was now beginning to change the culture of the inhabitants of Durham City.

Police of Spaces. The medicalization and hygienic transformation of family life in Durham City

In the nineteenth century, Durham City culture was producing disease in two ways. In a concrete way it began changing the ecology so that the risk of a particular disease could be reduced. In a semantic sense, culture also began to produce a theoretical system that enabled understanding and manipulation of disease - the system called medicine (Otto, 1993: 26). The many facets of public health; treatment and prevention of sickness, promotion of cleanliness etc., are loaded with cultural concerns of the kind related to Foucault's work. For Foucault, medicine and the medicalization of the population are seen as instruments in the states' struggle for sovereignty. Foucault calls medicine a 'life technique' because it is a state technique, which seeks to make every individual monitor their health and hygiene and arrange their daily life with a view to staying healthy and productive in a capitalist society. In terms of space, the study of different kinds of disease (medicine of species) was replaced by an interest in the environment, or rather in the causal relationship between surroundings and morbidity (medicine of spaces).

An example of the medicalisation of spaces can be seen in November 1854, when the Local Board of Health for the City of Durham gave the City's Common Corporate Seal to a list containing eighteen regulations relating to the management of Common Lodging Houses. Four days later, in Whitehall, London, the Prime Minister, Mr. Palmerston, confirmed these regulations as lawful. Subsequently, an Inspector of Common Lodging Houses for

Durham City was appointed to ensure the regulations were adhered to (DCRO, Durham City Council, Local Authority Records, Common Lodging Houses, Du3/14/1). The science of 'Lodging House Police' had arrived. Amongst the many rules for the medicalization of spaces undertaken by lodging house keepers, the inspector, usually the Police Superintendent, was to ensure:

> 1 The keeper shall not receive into the house or any room a greater number of lodgers or other persons fixed by the Local Board of Health, on the Report of their Inspector of Common Lodging Houses. The keeper shall display a ticket in each room showing how many persons are allowed in the room.
>
> 2 On notice from the Inspector of CLH keeper shall reduce and cease to receive or accommodate lodgers.
>
> 3 Two children under 8 to be counted as one lodger.
>
> 4 Kitchen and Scullery not to be used as sleeping apartments.
>
> 5 Rooms below the ground shall not be used as sleeping accommodation.
>
> 6 Unless married or members of family, children of opposite sexes shall not occupy the same rooms.
>
> 7 Keeper to keep the windows open to the full width of window from 9am-11am and from 2pm-4pm unless tempestuous weather or by illness of person in the room.

8 Floors to be swept thoroughly and washed thoroughly each Friday before 12 midday. Blankets, walls, rugs covers, to be cleansed four times a year. 'That is to say: At least once sometime during the First Week of each of the several Months of March, June, September, and December'.

9 Keeper to ventilate premises and to give notice immediately of any fever or infectious disease occurring.

10 Every house to be furnished with a dustbin of sufficient size to contain dust, ashes, garbage, offal, filth, and other refuse matter and clear away at least once a week.

11 Provide a water closet or privy – one closet or privy for every 20 persons.

12 The drains closets and sinks to be trapped.

13 The water closets to be kept clean – walls and floors etc.

14 The yards and areas of the LH shall be paved.

15 Every such lodging house shall have a proper drain communicating with the common sewer, where such sewer is within one hundred yards of the premises.

16 Provide satisfactory accommodation for cooking and washing.

17 Every room occupied as a sleeping apartment shall be furnished with sufficient bedsteads and bedding for the number of lodgers authorised to receive in such room.

18 The number of each sleeping room shall be legibly painted on the door thereof, and a corresponding number painted on the ticket intended for such room (DCRO Du3/14/1).

By 1855 seventy-three lodging houses had been registered in the city, of which twenty-six were in Framwellgate, five in Crossgate, eight in Claypath, three in South Street, two in Church Street, four in Gilesgate, three in Water Lane, twelve in New Elvet, three in Milburngate, two in Court Lane, one in Marketplace and one in Silver Street. Remarks recorded on regular inspections showed whether premises were, clean, mostly clean, or dirty.

The Irish were inherently associated with lodging houses, but not just as lodgers. Of the seventy-three, twenty-seven were registered by Irish named persons and these were mainly in Framwellgate and New Elvet. In Water Lane, for instance, in premises owned by Mrs. Jane Forster, Edward Kelly was registered as the keeper. The position of the rooms managed by Mr. Kelly were on the ground and first floors with others in a garret. The register recorded length, breadth, height, number of windows and whether they could be opened, together with details of an open chimney flu, number of beds in each room and whether mattresses were of chaff or feathers.

Administration of spaces included slaughterhouses. Bad water and disease is classless. This accounts for the general death rate, irrespective of the social location. In 1851 the health problems of Durham City were due mainly to a poor water supply and inadequate drainage of the sewage and other forms of effluence emanating from domestic and commercial premises such as slaughterhouses. An opposing view by Dr. Clark to the opinions of Drs. Oliver and Watkin. Dr. Clark had concluded that:

> .....the mortality of the city of Durham is excessive as compared with that of other towns, being nearly 30 in the 1000 annually, and that this mortality is closely connected with a serious deficiency of water supply and of drainage, of proper paving in the courts, and with a filthy and defective state of the conveniences of the poorer classes, and the presence of numerous open cesspools (Clark, 1849: 28).

Thus, a more scientific assessment rather than blaming it on the Irish and their supposed bad hygiene. Bye Laws made by the Local Board of Health of the Borough of Durham for the regulation of slaughterhouses amounted to Fourteen Bye Laws in all. 4 of these rules follow:

> 1 Occupier shall cause well ventilated, thoroughly whitewashed with quick lime at least four times a year,

namely: between 1st and 10th March and 1st and 10th
June and 1st and 10 September and 1st and 10th
December.

2 Keep a sufficient number of tubs, boxes, or vessels,
with tight and close fitting covers thereto, constructed
to the satisfaction of the officer of health, for the
purpose of receiving and conveying away all manure,
garbage, and filth, and shall, immediately after the
killing and dressing of any cattle ...cause all such
manure garbage and filth to be placed in such tubs,
boxes and vessels and ....together with their contents
shall be removed beyond the limits of the said Borough
of Durham.

3 No animal to be kept longer than 72 hours before
slaughter.

4 Shall not keep any ferocious dog unless securely
fastened or muzzled (DCRO Du 3/15/2).

Police of Highways

Framwellgate Bridge during this period was seen as of
insufficient width and strength to cater for the
increase of industrial traffic. As it is today, it crosses
the River Wear and provides the only access to Silver
Street and onward to the Marketplace. There had
been an agreement between the Durham
Commissioners and the Magistracy as to the
improvement of Framwellgate Bridge in 1826 and
1827. Durham Commissioners had laid the grievance

about the bridge before the Bench at the Christmas Quarter Sessions. In consequence of this communication the magistracy, on 1st. May 1827 submitted a plan called Number 2 for widening the bridge, to the consideration of the Commissioners. It was agreed to complete certain improvements suggested at the north end of the bridge as soon as funds and powers would allow.

On the 2nd. October 1827 the Commissioners ordered that so much of Mrs. Madgin's and Mr. Hopper Williamson's houses should be removed at the expense of the Commissioners. On 4th. March 1828 Mr. Bonomi, the County Surveyor, submitted to the Commissioners a plan for the widening of the bridge. In 1828 some improvements to the immediate approaches of the bridge were made by the Commissioners at a cost of about £1000. Work on the bridge widening, however, stalled and was not completed, but not forgotten.

A special meeting of the Local Board of Health for the district of the City of Durham was held in the Town hall on 24th. October 1855. And a report was presented by the Framwellgate Bridge Committee. The Committee unanimously adopted the following resolutions:

> 1 The bridge is …too narrow and insufficient for the present traffic, and passage over it.
>
> 2 The anticipated increase in traffic which will be caused by ……the completion of the Durham and Bishop Auckland Railway will render it highly dangerous, and wholly unfit for the accommodation of the public.
>
> 3 The County Council should be indicted for the described condition of the bridge.
>
> 4 The County Council pledged in 1828 to complete the widening and renovation of the bridge. The work that was commenced then should be continued and progressed.
>
> 5 A copy of the report has been handed to the magistrates at the Court of General Quarter Sessions.
>
> 6 The insufficiency of the bridge is admitted by all.
>
> 7 The preferring of the indictment shall not be seen as hostile act against the County Council.
>
> 8 It ought to be considered how further improvement can be effected in the approach to the bridge by widening certain areas of Silver Street which may be carried out at the same time as the widening by the bridge.

9 That the beauty and outline of the bridge be retained
after the renovation has taken place.

The report noted that the footpath on the east side of
Framwellgate Bridge was narrow at four feet, with no
footpath on the west side. The single path was
deemed insufficient for the large crowds, exposing
them to mud and carriage traffic. The roadway's
width varied from 18 feet at the south end to 14 feet
6 inches at the north end, which expanded to 25 feet
at the northern termination. The narrow limit was
criticized, especially as the law mandated a minimum
width of 20 feet for ordinary town approaches. The
imminent opening of a new railway between Bishop
Auckland and Durham was noted and that the bridge
was the sole access to the station and its traffic. This
would have been Gilesgate Station as the present
main line station was not opened until 1857. The
report notes that Gilesgate Station handled about
34,000 tons of merchandise traffic annually, with an
additional 5,000 tons for minerals, lime, and stone.
Passengers were estimated at 2,800 per week, served
by 20 cabs and 150 omnibuses. The plea was made to
widen the bridge, as begun in 1828 in order to

accommodate the growing traffic and impending
railway connection. (9th. August 1849 – 7th. May 1862.
Special Meeting of the Local Board of Health
24.10.1855. DCRO Du 3/1/1).

In 1855 the council had employed, 'proper parties' to
carry out a survey of traffic on the bridge and they
reported results as follows:

> Saturday, October 13th. From 6am to 10pm.
> Foot passengers 22,849; Sheep 65; Oxen 42; Carriages
> 649; Horses 566.
>
> Monday October 15th. From 6am to 10 pm.
> Foot Passengers 9,271; Sheep 65; Carriages 446; Horses
> 211.

Statistics and Power

For Foucault, statistics and surveillance go hand in
hand. As Hacking notes, historically, the collection of
statistics has created, at the least, a great bureaucratic
machine. It may think of itself as providing only
information, but 'it is itself part of the technology of
power in a modern state' (Hacking, 1991: 181-196). In
Foucault's historiography, surveillance is part of
governmental practices aimed at producing certain

136

sorts of persons. In the case of the empirical vigilance carried out on Framwellgate Bridge, this was part of a process to ensure a successful application for improvement to the widening of the bridge. In turn, this assisted in producing residents as maximized citizens, able to adapt to rapid development and maximize the capitalist project through easier highway access to the market.

Durham City as a medicalizable object

Foucault focuses upon control of the body through the medium of rational, systematic knowledge (Foucault, 1963, 1981: 125). In respect of medicine, with the introduction of inoculation and vaccination we learn of a new administrative emphasis on:

> ....the family as the most constant agent of medicalisation (Foucault, 1981: 172-173).

Hygiene was supplemented with a grander programme as the development of 'homo hygienicus' involved a regime of health for whole populations. This entailed a certain number of authoritarian

administrative and medical interventions and controls
where:

> …. the city with its spatial variables (came to
> appear) as a medicalizable object' (Foucault
> 1980: 175).

Foucault suggests that this was a dual project. It
involved firstly, the indefinite extension of strength,
vigour, health, and life, existing at a more macro-level
in the service of the economy, especially the
dominance of the bourgeoisie (Foucault, 1981: 125).
The second element of the project concerned the
presence of a physical aspect, evident in the works
published in great numbers at the end of the
eighteenth century on body hygiene, the art of
longevity, ways of having healthy children and of
keeping them alive as long as possible, and methods
for improving the human lineage (Foucault, 1981:
125). The health and hygiene project which was
taking place in nineteenth century Durham City was a
cautiously 'experimental' response to historically
located problems of the moral training of the
population which emerged from a tradition which was

closely connected to science (Kendall and Wickham, 1999: 124).

8 CONCLUSIONS

The data presented here would tend to show that the mid-Victorian Durham Irishman did fit the stereotype of Drunken, Wild, Violent and Dishonest, but this was not over-represented in the local press. Indeed, more current study of this subject area has shown that similar tendencies of the Irish to those prevalent in the Victorian period continue today (Lambert, 1970). But, in sensibly rejecting the philosophy of scientific racism as a legitimate theory as to why there were high levels of Irish crime in mid-Victorian Durham, there is a need to provide a more balanced explanation of these findings. Crime rates in rural Ireland were and are very low (ibid). Close-knit family life and the strong influence of the Catholic Church may well exert potent controls over wrong-doing and law breaking. But it is not unlikely that in many cases the process of immigration removes these controlling influences. For those Irish immigrants who did not find economic security, stable family relations and other signs of success in mid-Victorian Durham, the release of the stringent controls of the home society may have found expression in relatively greater crime and disorder. Failure means poor living conditions and poor occupational attainment in areas where overcrowding and disorganization were common, and the corollary was crime and disorder. It has been found that relatively more Irish immigrants fail in these terms than other immigrants or similarly placed English persons. So, it may not be surprising that the Irish were over-represented among the urban poor and thus over-represented among the ranks of offenders (Lambert, op. cit: 127).

Accordingly, apart from any inherent personal criminal tendencies, the Irish criminal in mid-Victorian Durham must be viewed in relation to that specific historical epoch where certain social, economic, political and religious conditions prevailed, for each of these had a bearing on, to some degree, the total criminal involvement. It is very likely that a major part of the cause of a high crime rate amongst Irish immigrants in County Durham stemmed from the fact that they may well have provided a large part of the population which was at risk of being involved in most criminal activity - youthful, unskilled or semiskilled and living in areas of poor accommodation. Indeed, it is an accepted fact that these are the characteristics of most persons who find themselves in the criminal statistics today.

So, migration, like all other forms of change, involves risk. The experience of upheaval for the Durham Irish immigrant, and the inadequate preparation given by one cultural background for life in another, gave rise to problematic situations. It is very likely that many of the weaknesses which were exposed by the Irish immigrant situation in Durham were weaknesses in the fabric, structure, and ideology of the host nation. The situation is the same today - pressures of change represented by immigrants in Britain express and threaten the weaknesses of the British people

(Police Monitoring and Research Group 1988). Accordingly, there is a need for studies of immigrant communities not to be carried out in isolation from studies of the host society nor divorced from consideration of the continuing influence of past origins. Research into the social condition of the Irish, or any other immigrant group, must therefore be carried out in relation to the total familiarity of the cultural, historical, and social aspects of their personal experience.

Turning to comparisons of social class in Durham City, when we consider the contrasting views of commentators on the 'new' police and the new administration of the population, they effectively provide a 'developmental' view of history which leaves them open to a charge of being 'ahistorical'. They assume the inevitability of their thesis and tend to ignore the possibility of other explanations. Although it is helpful as a research device to place two competing theories into ideal-typical paradigms which produce dichotomies of social order in terms of whether consensus or coercion exists, these ideal-types are merely theoretically created and lack an empirical basis. It is hoped, therefore, that the value of the present study is in the empirical basis of the comparison it has provided.

The Surveillance of Society

In British society order can be understood as based either upon the consent of the vast majority or largely by coercion - subtle or blatant - of the majority by a powerful minority. This study demonstrates clearly that the Durham City Borough Police of the period existed primarily to protect the institutions of private property and enforce statutory norms of public order which were mainly designed to ensure the free circulation of commodities and satisfy the minority bourgeoisie population's concerns of the time. Accordingly, there is a sense in which the 'private' nature of policing in Durham City continued to prevail well after the 'public' policing system was installed in 1836. Durham City's 'public' police were public in name only. Classicism's view of order in mid-Victorian society emphasized the importance of private property, just rewards for entrepreneurial skill

and the right to accumulate wealth. This produced a
social structure in which the basis of rights and
benefits was very unequally distributed throughout
society. The rights which the law protected stemmed
from, and ultimately reverted to, the individual citizen
who was seen as the foundation of social order. But
equivalence could not be squeezed out of the poor of
Durham City; clearly shown here by the fact they
were not receiving equal policing provision and were
probably considered as subjects of a complaint rather
than subjects making one. And they must have had
many to make. For instance, where were the
complaints of domestic violence which the Durham
Police in contemporary times are regularly called to
deal with? One answer must be that the poor's 'stake'
in law and order was effectively constrained by their
limited economic and political power. Their own
perception of this reality must surely have restricted
their options in calling the police when the need arose
(Ignatieff, 1979: 144).

Although recognizing that today's society is still
dominated by what is now a neo-classical model of

law and order, official police records since the mid-Victorian period show clearly that the police are now overwhelmed with complaints from the less well-off. This may not be so surprising when we consider the social, economic, and political progress which that section of society has made since the 1860's.

The advent of modern medicine brought about coherent developments in various fields, including architecture. Foucault (1979) highlights the application of architectural design in institutionalized settings, particularly in prisons and hospitals. This design mirrored scientific developments in control and surveillance techniques, encompassing the management and observation of entire populations, such as census data, epidemiology, and demographic registers, and the scrutiny of individual bodies through advances in clinical medicine and anatomy. This architectural approach originated from Jeremy Bentham's concept of the Panopticon, designed for maximum supervision with minimal effort (Foucault 1980). The Panopticon's surveillance potential fosters self-discipline, leading individuals to 'gaze upon themselves,' and this self-discipline replaces torture as the definitive method of social control.

Foucault's examination of the evolution of disciplinary society provides insights into the factors paving the way for an administrative transformation across every institution within Durham society. The medicalization and hygienic transformation of family life in Durham City had commenced in the late eighteenth century. Under the principles of medical police, the city became a crucial site for medical reasoning and techniques. Early police practices aimed at comprehensive knowledge and visibility of the governed population, regulated in detail from the weight of bread to Sabbath attire. Though remnants of this approach persist, the nineteenth century saw a shift towards a more liberal form of health governance. This entailed purifying the 'public' domain through town planning to eliminate disease in dark areas while regulating, rather than restricting, freedom in 'private' spaces for the health of the social body (Rose, 1994).

An interest in finding the possible causes of disease was already flourishing in the eighteenth century. At the same time, doctors were given an administrative role, since they had to report to the government about the medical profile of the population, that is, about disease, causes of death, fertility, and so on, in relation to the topographical conditions. It can be said that at this time there was a completely new medical/administrative discourse. Medical topographies were an early form of describing folk life, and as such they helped to construct the concept of nation, the idea of a people as a group of individuals with their own shared characteristics and regularities. Medicine first helped to create the concept of a people, and then it became interested in what was going on among this people as regards disease. As Otto puts it, 'Self-interest and concern for health become guiding factors in everyday life (Otto, 1993).

EPILOUGE.

POLICING: FROM THE SURVEILLANCE OF SOCIETY TO THE SOCIETY OF SURVEILLANCE

For many, there is something sacred about traditional institutions discussed in earlier chapters - the constabulary police service and the health service. In contemporary social change, these traditional institutions have now become 'de-institutionalised' according to Giddens (Giddens, 1971), that is to say, they have been hollowed out or they appear culturally reduced from their older form. Through a series of policy changes over time, a dis-embedding and re-embedding process has, and continues to occur to such bodies which radically changes them as institutions and requires the possibility of a semantic change from their traditional identity. In this prologue I will set out some general ways these changes have occurred to the health service and the police service and will then provide a more detailed analysis of this concept of de-institutionalisation based on my personal experiences as a detective officer in Durham Constabulary.

Together

The primary de-institutionalization of the National Health Service (NHS) involves a departure from the traditional healthcare model centred on large institutions like hospitals, towards a more community-oriented and patient-centric approach. Key strategies contributing to this shift include the expansion of community-based care, emphasizing preventive measures, promoting outpatient services, reforming mental health services towards community-based care, enhancing the integration of health and social care, utilizing technology for remote healthcare delivery, and empowering patients in their own care decisions. These changes aim to provide more personalized, accessible, and patient-focused healthcare. To represent this idea today, the Scottish region of the NHS has a branding emblem which says simply, 'Together'.

Better Together

The evolution and de-institutionalisation of the constabulary police has led to a comprehensive understanding of 'police' beyond the traditional state police concept. Applying Giddens' concepts, the transformation of policing practices is evident in the adoption of flexible, community-oriented strategies. Technological advancements contribute to a shift in perceptions of time and space, allowing for more rapid and decentralized police responses. In this evolution, no longer does the state take full responsibility for policing but the liberal democratic idea of citizen's 'responsibilization' takes effect. In the Durham Constabulary of the present day this is summed up in the force's emblem which says, 'Better Together'.

Reflexive modernization, as Giddens observes it, occurs through continuous policy reassessment and reform, emphasizing community engagement and transparency. The professionalization and specialization of policing, particularly in areas like cybercrime and counterterrorism, reflect Giddens' notion of 'expert systems'. Community policing models, highlighting individual agency and tailored responses, signify a move away from a constant institutional approach. While Giddens' ideas help us understand these changes, however, it is crucial to acknowledge the multifaceted nature of deinstitutionalization in policing.

Furthermore, it is not necessarily to say that traditional forms like these change so much that they become lost in memory. Accordingly, in his thesis on institutional reflexivity and expert systems, Giddens claims that in the post-traditional order traditions do not wholly disappear - they may remain as 'Relics' (Giddens, 1994: 100-103). Thus, seventy-five years after his first appearance in the TV series *Dixon of Dock Green*, its hero, PC George Dixon, for many, still remains symbolically representative of what the British Police should be today – venerated, culturally unique national heroes (Reiner, 1992: 761).

But public attitudes towards the police in Britain have changed dramatically since PC Dixon was first on the beat in the 1950's. Many other symbols of the so-called 'Golden Age' of policing have also become a memory - locked away like 'Relics' in the 'living museum' of policing as 'The Police' experiences these de-institutionalising processes:

> Artefacts once associated with both great and little traditions in the post-traditional order tend to become relics, although should be extended to cover more than only physical objects. A 'relic', as I use the word here, covers any item in a living museum. Relics are not just objects or practices which happen to live on residue of traditions that have become weakened or lost; they are invested with meaning as exemplars of a transcended past......Relics are signifiers of a past which has no development or at least whose causal connections to the

present are not part of what gives them their identity (Giddens, 1994: 102).

It is in that sense that Giddens uses the term 'shell institutions'.

Finally, there is an argument that the apparent diminishing of sovereignty in policing services strengthens the police organization rather than weakens its sovereignty. As danger increases and people become more fearful, communities tend to separate. In response to the public's fear of crime, the police take on the role of collecting and sharing information, thereby reinforcing their function in maintaining order and safety. So, importantly, as I will show in a practical and personal example later, Giddens and others point out that the notion of the nation-state losing its powers is a contested one (Giddens, 1987). He claims that Globalization is not a process which naturally diminishes sovereign power, on the contrary, it is part of the chief condition of the world-wide extension of the nation-state system in current times (Giddens, 1987: 304). Indeed, the neoliberal agenda has benefited from this in the form of widespread privatisation of policing services as public provision of services moves from fate to choice (McManus, 1995).

Responsibilization of the public

Institutional reflexivity in the police organisation can be said to have been taking place over time and its effects were especially evident around 1998 with the introduction of The Crime and Disorder Act of that year. It involves the transformation of expert systems, which the police traditionally provided, into democratically dialogical and political public spheres, e.g. community safety partnerships. This is what the Crime and Disorder Act effectively required in law. According to Giddens, institutional reflexivity entails increased democracy – 'dialogical avowal' of responsibility by the police, as Giddens would put it. 'Avowal' meaning 'acknowledgement'. In the case of community safety, therefore, the nature of policing in communities should be a matter not merely for the police but for the whole community. Increasingly, the police are sharing their expertise with other agencies. In this sense one would expect the nature of policing to become more democratic over time.

Accordingly, as the result of a combination of globalisation and the transformation of everyday life, Giddens recognises four social contexts in which democratising processes are at work. Firstly, the potential emergence of Emotional Democracy - parent-child and friendship relations. For policing purposes, we can see here also the individual 'security customer'. The trends in the replacement of bureaucratic hierarchies by more flexible and decentralised systems of authority is also recognized by Giddens. We are prompted to consider 'government at a distance' here and the notion of 'responsibilization' of their own security by the public, who had once upon a time looked totally for this towards the police. The development of social movements and self-help groups have also developed rapidly. For our purposes, a simple example here is Neighbourhood Watch. Finally, more democratic influences at the global levels of development have occurred in contemporary society. Here we can see the influence of government philosophies such as New Localism and Neighbourhood Policing.

For Giddens, therefore, it is as if the traditional police are being washed away on a tide of dialogical avowal as we are freed from traditions like 'the police' institution, which ends up metaphorically like an empty shell. Yet, as previously mentioned and according to Beck, such institutions will not die, they become 'Zombie Institutions' which are dead but are unable to die (Beck, 1997: 140) and must re-invent themselves. So, this has particular relevance to policing in the late modern era, evoking thoughts of the Crime and Disorder Act, 1998 and Community Safety Partnerships and the police organization apparently hanging on to sovereignty as expectations of more democracy in policing derive in the public's psyche.

Although the police institution today may look different than in the Victorian period, the social characteristics of complainants and targets in Victorian Durham City seems relatively unchanged. There has been, however, an increase in the numbers of the better off while the poor exist in an environment of shrinking employment and greater dependence on welfare. Of course, we see greater policing technology in the city in the form of cameras and parking metres. But they are no less designed for social control than those at an earlier period, and, as before, the strategies for them are usually coordinated nationally, i.e. the Home Office.

Having provided the foregoing analysis of change, I want to argue Giddens and Becks point that these traditional and individually powerful institutions still hold sway in many ways. I will focus here on one aspect of this, police culture, and use the traditional detective as an example from my own experience and show to some extent that the traditional culture prevails today and that it is much deeper seated than local institutions reveal.

My own reflective experiences tell me that a hint of the old dominant association with the established church, and an obsessive and elitist nationalism in recruiting officers persists today in the organization, nationally. Perhaps the religious connection would not have been so surprising in Victorian times, but surely not in the multi-cultural society of today, where it is especially important for the institution to be representative of all the people being policed.

It is true that a change in culture across the whole spectrum of society has improved recruiting of ethnic minority officers into the constabulary police, but the change is still not drawing enough into the force - and those who do join often discover a racist element in some of their colleagues. In this respect, the very need for a national association to consider the interests of black police officers, The Black Police Association, says much about the present police culture.

The Veneration and Death of the Traditional Detective?

Traditions usually have guardians - wise men, priests, sages. These were institutional experts in pre-modern communities. If traditions persisted in institutions, then people turned to experts and the primary crime controllers were traditional detectives. It could be easily argued that police professionalism and expertise in community safety has diminished in late modern society. It is claimed by some that crime is now an everyday risk to be managed like air pollution and road traffic and consequentially brings with it the erosion of one of the foundational myths of modern society; that the sovereign state is capable of providing security, law and order and crime control.

The description of the police as a 'relic' is far from the one I was introduced to as a new recruit to the Durham Constabulary in 1971. The experts and guardians of crime control then were the divisional detectives – traditional heroes like George Dixon. The police force that I joined was clearly an organisation which had singularity of function,

160

individual freedom, and personal autonomy as part of the CID ethos. These characteristics seem hardly observable five decades later, swamped as they have been in a plethora of new policy implementation that has affected great change, not only administrative procedures but the occupational culture itself. This began happening while I was a serving officer.

On joining the Durham force, I was very aware of an elitist class of officer to whom I immediately aspired – the divisional detective. I use the detective officer as an example here of institutional reflexivity and change. He, the detective; and it was invariably a male domain in those days, knew himself to be a clear reflection of effective police work. He knew the law of theft and offences against the person particularly well. He was an accepted member of the local community in which he worked and prided himself on knowing what was going on there. A proven investigator and interviewer he had the ability to charm, persuade or, if necessary, intimidate those from whom he required information or confessions. Invariably he was an energetic producer of detected crimes and a manipulator of national statistics. If he was clever enough, he was able to control the volume of his work in order to spend more time visiting licensed premises on his 'patch' and speak to informants while seeking 'pints of information', as my wife termed it. The limited professional worth of such public house visits was retained as a departmental confidence and used as a cloak in which to protect his professional mystery and mastery. And he was a master in his own right and very aware that his success was primarily due to his individual ability, personality, and energy. Importantly, his success required a complete acceptance of the occupational culture existing within the organization.

For young police officers like me aspiring to the CID in the 1970's there was a sense too in which detectives were both 'made' and 'accepted' by their peer group. A good part of this concerned taking on the cultural baggage, which came with the kudos of being on the CID. Selected for an interview for transfer to the CID early in my career, in the tradition of 'surprise' which all good interviewers understand, I was asked by the

Detective Chief Superintendent (God) 'Why do you think you'll make a detective son?' 'An ability to cope with the investigation and detection of high volumes of reported crime' was a fundamental and expected answer. But importantly, the interviewer crucially needed to know whether I understood, and could be trusted to take on, the occupational culture of the CID. Paradoxically, in order to become the 'autonomous individual detective' there was a need to lose some personal individuality by taking on the group values too.

Like rank, such professionalism and culture requires its own real and symbolic boundaries and space. The CID Office has a particular place here. Always 'upstairs' and nearer to God, it was an enclave of mystery to me and the majority of my young-in-service uniform colleagues. A nervous sensation of being in the company of an occupational power-elite increased as you proceeded further up the CID staircase towards the office. The office was the centre of excellence in the investigation and detection of crime – the apparent powerhouse of effective crime control.

The success of the force in combating crime was, accordingly, in no small part the result of the detective's individual effort and much of the success was seen to be in his hands. A sense of sharing this responsibility with the uniform department was never seriously contemplated as policy – for a start, you could not trust a uniform man to take the kind of professional risks a detective was prepared to take for the sake of 'detected' crime. 'Economical truth' was a cultural trait of the CID, as were other devices of detection such as 'uneconomical intimidation'. These were not in the nature of dyed in the wool uniform personnel. These were times when you could leave your un-admitting prisoner in the cells for long periods of solitary confinement without having to account to the custody officer in charge of the prisoners – an ideal softener for confessions.

The CID response to crime was total – every reported crime was investigated to some degree. And what was recorded officially in the crime book was primarily a matter for the CID. Although the crime book was available to the uniform department for recording purposes, CID officers strictly monitored what was, and was not recorded. They were the guardians of the figures, which had to reflect success rather than failure at any manipulative cost. This culture of manipulated success existed extensively throughout the organization. No room here for the statistical uncertainties of today's community crime prevention or for sharing professional knowledge and power. Of course, this was not just a culture on the ground. It was an endemic culture which received the nod and the wink of the highest officers in the force and officials in the Home Office.

The 1970's, 80's and 90's, and indeed today, reveal more about the police culture and professional shortcomings than the police would have wished. Corruption, malpractice and injustices, racial and sexual discrimination, and harassment and, importantly, ineffectiveness at controlling crime are just some of the problems the police have to face. A decline in the annual proportion of crimes cleared up, from approximately 47 per cent during the 1950s to an early 2000s figure of around 38 per cent seems hardly a recipe for success. This decline in the level of police effectiveness over the recent past is compounded by evidence which shows not only decreasing levels of police detection but increasing levels of unreported crime and increasing levels of government spending on policing.

Culture Busters

Set against a backdrop of recurring public expenditure squeeze, police reform was inevitable in the 1990s. Enter the powerful 'culture busters'. The Police and Criminal Evidence Act and the policy of New Public Management are a few examples of legislation and government policy that was designed to literally bust the old crime-busters' culture of local autonomy. In 1996 the Audit Commission published a report on crime management stating that, traditional departmentalism had been an impediment in galvanising the entire force in successful control of crime. It confirmed the occupational culture of crime detection rather than crime prevention and stated that the public would prefer a low crime rate rather than a high detection rate.

A Crime Strategy was needed. Recommendations, such as a clear crime management structure which would include Crime Desks, freeing up detectives' time to investigate more serious crime by, paradoxically, designating the uniform constable as the initial investigator of the less serious offences with individual responsibility for the whole investigation, and a proactive rather than a reactive approach to crime management, are now implemented fully in all forces in England and Wales. The rationality which New Public Management and its tools, like the Audit Commission, brings to policing, and in turn the public, must surely of course be a good thing.

Survival of Traditional Culture

Almost three decades after joining the force, as the force Crime Strategy Coordinator I spoke once a month to probationer constables about the finer points of the force's Crime Strategy and told them how the old detective went about his duty in the 1970's and 80's, until the Audit Commission proposed changes. I continually experienced a state of Deja vu when being told by my audience that their impressions of the CID as powerful and elitist is still the same and that time, policy and procedures have not made that much difference to the culture of the organization. Accordingly, in this respect the CID appears a 'shell' institution; the relic that Giddens describes, but its traditional cultural form has not died. Change certainly has had impact, but perhaps not yet to the degree required. I am reminded of the Lawrence Enquiry and the earlier failed policy implementation derived from another grand enquiry which should have avoided that disgrace - The Scarman Report. According to uniform officers, they are clearly still outsiders in an occupational community which, like the concept of contemporary community itself, has many communities and cultures within it. Both the police and the community are victims of a culture. How to bring these cultures together – galvanise them – as the Audit Commission describes it, is clearly easier said than done.

BIBLIOGRAPHY

Alison, A. 1840 'Principles of Population', London, publisher unknown.

Banham, J. 1994 'A very great public conveniency: The origins of banking in County Durham', *Durham County Local History Society Bulletin,* 52, May:19-41.

Butler, D. 1992 'Durham City. The 1851 Census', Durham Historical Enterprises.

Byrne, D. 1998 'Complexity Theory and The Social Sciences: An Introduction', London, Routledge.

Canny, N.P. 1973 'The Ideology of English Colonisation: From England to America' in *William and Mary Quarterly,* 3rd series.

Cherbuliez, A. 1826 'Precis de la science economique et de ses principales applications', Vol. 2, Paris.

Census, Durham City, 1851; Marriage Records, St. Cuthbert's Roman Catholic Church, Elvet, Durham City.

Cilliers, P. 1998 'Complexity and Postmodernism: Understanding Complex Systems', London: Routledge.

Clark G.T. 1849 'Report to the General Board of Health on a Preliminary Enquiry into the Sewerage, Drainage, and supply of Water, and the Sanitary Condition of the Inhabitants of the Borough of Durham', London, Clowes and Sons.

Clifton, R. 1984 'The Popular Fear of Catholics in England, 1640-1660' in P. Slack (ed.), *Rebellion, Popular Protest and Social Order in Early Modern England,* London, Cambridge University Press.

Cohen, S. 1980, 'Folk Devils and Moral Panics: The Creation of the Mods and Rockers', London, MacGibbon and Kee.

Connell, P. Cronin, D. A. and O' Dalaigh, B. (eds.) 1998 'Irish Townlands: Studies in Local History', Dublin, Four Courts Press.

Cooter, R.J. 1972 'The Irish in County Durham and Newcastle, 1840-1880', unpublished M.A. Thesis no.156, University of Durham.

Cranfield, R. 1993 'Education for the 'Dangerous Classes' in Mid-Nineteenth Century Durham', in *Durham County Local History Society* Bulletin 50: 70-80.

Critchley, T.A. 1978, 'A History of the Police in England and Wales', London, Constable.

Darwin, C. 1871 'Descent of Man', London, John Murray.

DCRO Durham City Council, Local Authority Records, Common Lodging Houses, Du3/14/1.

Durham City Borough Police, Superintendent's Annual Report to the Watch Committee for year ending 29.9.1860. Durham County Record Office (DCRO) Ref. Du1/59/233.

Durham City Borough Police, Superintendent's Annual Report 31.5.1876, of the Watch Committee 31.5.1876. DCRO, Ref. Du1/59/125-142.

Feheney, J.M. 1983 'Delinquency Among Irish Children in Victorian London' in *Irish Historical Studies,* vol.23.

Finnigan, F. 1986 'The Irish in York' in S. Gilley and R. Swift (eds.), *The Irish in the Victorian City,* London, Croom Helm.

First Report of the Commissioners, 1836. The evidence of Dr. John Duke of Mohill, in First Report of the Commissioners for Inquiring into the condition of the Poorer Classes in Ireland,

Supplement to Appendix D.H.C., 1836, Vol. XXX1: Supplement to Appendix E.H.C., 1836, Vol. XXX11.

Foucault, M. 1963 'The Birth of the Clinic', London: Tavistock.

Foucault, M. 1975 'Discipline and Punish: The Birth of the Prison', New York, Pantheon.

Foucault, M. 1980 'Power/Knowledge', edited by C. Gordon, London, Harvester.

Foucault, M. 1981 'The History of Sexuality: An Introduction', London, Penguin.

Giddens, A. 1971 'Modernity and Self Identity, Self and Society in the Late Modern Age', Stanford, Calif., Stanford University Press.

Giddens, A. 1987 'Social Theory and Modern Sociology', Stanford, Calif., Stanford University Press.

Giddens, A., Beck, U. and Lash, S. 1994 'Reflexive Modernization: Politics, Tradition and Aesthetics in the Modern Social Order', Stanford, Calif., Stanford University Press.

Gilley, S. 1985 'The Irish' in *History Today*, vol.35: 16-23.

Gilley, S and Swift, H. 1986 'The Irish in the Victorian City', London, Croom Helm.

Gooch, L. 1993 'Papist Head-Hunting in County Durham, 1705-1851', *Durham County Local History Society Bulletin,* Vol. 50.

Hacking, I. 1991 'How should we do the history of statistics?' in Burchell G., Gordon C. and Miller P., 'The Foucault Effect: Studies in Governmentality' with two lectures and an interview with Michel Foucault, pp. 181-195. London, Harvester Wheatsheaf.

Hall, S. 1978 'Policing the Crisis: Mugging, The State and Law and Order', London, MacMillan.

Harvey, D. and Reed, M.H. 1994 'The Evolution of Dissipative Social Systems', *Journal of Social and Evolutionary Systems*, 17, 4: 371-411.

Harvey, D.L. and Reed, M.H. 1996 'Social Science as the Study of Complex Systems' in L. D. Kiel and E. Elliott (eds.), *Chaos Theory in the Social Sciences: Foundations and Applications*, Ann Arbor: The University of Michigan Press. pp. 295-323.

Heesom, A.J. 1992 'The Founding of the University of Durham,' Durham Cathedral Lecture 1992.

Ignatieff, M. 1979, 'Police and People: the birth of Mr. Peel's blue locusts', in *New Society*, 30th. August.

Ignatieff, M. 1981 'The ideological origins of the penitentiary' *Crime and Society, Readings in History and Theory,* pp-37-59, Fitzgerald, M, McLennan, G. and Pawson, J. (eds) London, Routledge.

Irving, E. 1829, 'The Last Days: A Discourse on the Evil Character of these Our Times', London; Seeley and Burnside.

Jones, W.R. 1971 'England Against the Celtic Fringe: A Study in Cultural Stereotypes' in *Journal of World History*, vol.13.

Kendall, G. and Wickham, G. 1999 'Using Foucault's Methods', London, Sage.

Krannich, R.S. and Greide, T.R. 1990.'Rapid Growth Effects on Rural Community Relations,' in Luloff, A.E. and Swanson, L. E. (Eds.), *American Rural Communities*. Boulder, Westview Press.

Mac Atasney, G. 1997 'Leitrim and the Great Hunger: A Temporary Inconvenience?', Carrick on Shannon, Carrick on Shannon and District Historical Society.

McCollum, M. 1973 *The Backhouse Papers*, GB-0033-BAC. Available online at: http://flambard.dur.ac.uk:6336/dynaweb/handlist/fam/bkhouse/

Lambert, E.M. 1970 'Crime, Police and Race Relations: A Study in Birmingham', London, Oxford University Press.

Lecky W.H. 1982 'A History of Ireland in the Eighteenth Century', London, Longmans, Green and Company.

Lindley, K.J. 1972 'The Impact of the 1641 Rebellion Upon England and Wales, 1641-1645' in *Irish Historical Studies,* 18: 143-176.

Lombroso, C. 1876 'L'Uomo Delinquente', Turin, Boca.

Lucas, E.V. 1925 'Playtime and Company, A Book for Children', London, Methuen.

Mayhew, H. 1981 'On the number of costermongers and other street folk', in Fitzgerald, M. McLennan, G. and Pawson, J. (eds) *Crime and Society: Readings in History and Theory*, London, Routledge.

Marx, K. and Engels, F. 1962, 'The Condition of the Working Class in England', Moscow.

McDonnell, F. 1991 'The Irish in Durham City, 1841-1861' *Durham County Local History Society Bulletin,* 47: 68-82.

McManus, M. 1989 'The Irish, how deviant?: Criminological perspectives on images and social control', unpublished dissertation, University of Northumbria.

McManus, M. 1995 'From Fate to Choice: Private Bobbies, Public Beats', Avebury.

Norris, P. 1984 'The Irish in Tow Law, Co. Durham, 1851-1871' in *Durham County Local History Society Bulletin,* 33: 41-70.

O'Hara, B. and Ómuraíle, N. 2002. *County Mayo: An Outline History,* available online at: http://www.mayo-ireland.ie/Mayo/History/FullHist.ht

Oliver, N. 1848 'Report on the Common Lodging Houses in the city of Durham', quoted in Clark G.T. 1849 *Report to the General Board of Health on a Preliminary Enquiry into the Sewerage, Drainage, and supply of Water, and the Sanitary Condition of the Inhabitants of the Borough of Durham,* London, Clowes and Sons.

Otto, L. 1993 'Medicine, Disease and Culture' Ethnologia Scandinavica, Vol. 23: 25-34.

Palatinate of Durham, Wikipedia https://en.wikipedia.org/wiki/County_Palatine_of_Durham#:~:text=It%20was%20built%20by%20Robert,Bedlington%2C%20Norham%2C%20and%20Craycke. Accessed 9.12.2023.

Pasquino, P. 1978 'Theatrum Politicum. The Genealogy of Capital - Police and the State of Prosperity', *Ideology and Consciousness*, 4: 41-54.

Paz, D.J. 1986 'Anti-Catholicism, Anti-Irish Stereotyping and Anti-Celtic Racism in Mid-Victorian Working Class Periodicals', *Albion*, 18: 601-616.

Pearson, G. 1983 'Hooligan: A history of Respectable Fears', London, MacMillan.

Police Monitoring and Research Group 1988, 'Policing and the Irish Community', Briefing Paper no.5.

Prigogine, I. and Stengers, I. 1984 'Order Out of Chaos,' New York, Bantam.

Procacci, G. 1991 'Social economy and the government of Poverty' in Burchell G., Gordon C. and Miller P., *The Foucault Effect: Studies in Governmentality with two lectures and an interview with Michel Foucault*, pp. 151-168, pp. 158-164, London, Harvester Wheatsheaf.

Radzinowicz, L. 1968 'A History of English Criminal Law and its Administration from 1750', Vol 3, London, Stevens and Sons.

Richardson, E.G. 1938 'English Institutions in Medieval Ireland' in *Irish Historical Studies,* vol. 1.

Otway-Ruthven, I. 1950 'The Request of the Irish for English Law' in *Irish Historical Studies,* vol. 6.

Redfield, R. 1947 'The Folk Society', American Journal of Sociology, 52, 3: 293-308.

Redfield, R. 1968 'The Primitive World and its Transformations'. Harmonsworth, Penguin.

Reid, D.B. 1845 *Durham, Report on its Sanatory Conditions in Second report of the Commissioners for Inquiring into the State of Large Towns.* Parliamentary Papers 1845: 610 xviii.

Reiner, R. 1992 'Policing a Postmodern Society', *The Modern Law Review* 55, 6: 761-781.Wiley.

Roncati, A. 1985 'Petty. The Origins of Political Economy', translated by Isabella Cherubini. Cardiff, University College, Cardiff Press.

Rose, N. 1994 'Medicine, History and the Present', in Jones, C. and Porter, R. (eds) 'Reassessing Foucault: Power, Medicine and the Body', London, Routledge.

Shaw, G. 1868 *A Statistical Table of the Mortality of the City of Durham: For Eighteen Years and Three Months, ending the 31ˢᵗ. March, 1859*. DCRO D/CL 1, adapted in *Durham, 1849, Public Health Act, Report to the General Board of Health on Durham 1849,* 1997 Durham County Local History Society, with an introduction by David Butler, p. viii.

Stein, M.R. 1960 'The Eclipse of Community', Princeton, Princeton University Press.

Swift, R., 1984, 'Anti-Catholicism and Irish disturbances: Public Order in Mid-Victorian Wolverhampton', in *Midland History*, 9: 87-108.

Swift, R.,1986, 'Another Stafford Street Row: Law and Order and the Irish presence in Mid-Victorian Wolverhampton', in *Immigrants and Minorities in British Society,* Holmes, C. (ed) pp. 5-29, London, George Allen and Unwin.

The Devon Commission. Report of the Commissioners of Inquiry into the Law and Practice in Respect of the Occupation of Land in Ireland. Digest of Evidence, Part 1, H.C., 1845 (605) Vol. X1X, Evidence of Theophilous Jones of Drumard.

The Devon Commission, 1845, Witness 448. Evidence taken from witness 448, before Her Majesty's Commissioners of Inquiry into the state of the law and practice in respect to the occupation of land in Ireland.

Thompson, E.P. 1968 'The Making of the English Working Class' London, Penguin.

Tonnies, F. 1957 'Community and Society', New York, Harper and Row.

Watson, A.S. and Harrison, D. 1990 'Policing the Land of the Prince Bishops: The History of Durham Constabulary, 1840-1990', Durham Books.

Weld, I. 1832 'Statistical Survey of the county Roscommon', Dublin, and Lewis, G.C. 1836: 71, 'On local disturbances in Ireland and on the Irish Church question' London.

Whellan, F. 1894 'History, Topography and Directory of the County Palatinate of Durham.

White, Captain W. 1838 'Police Spy, or the Metropolitan Police; its advantages, abuses, and defects', London, Strange.

Williams, R. 1983 'Keywords: A Vocabulary of Culture and Society', London, Fontana Press.

Young, J. 1981 'Thinking Seriously about Crime' in, *Crime and Society, Readings in History and Theory,* Fitzgerald, M., McLennan, G and Pawson, J. (eds).

Zedner, L. 2009 'Security' London, Routledge.

INDEX

A

a report was presented by the
    Framwellgate Bridge
    Committee · 134
Anarchic Celt threatening the
    young girl Hibernia · 35
Anti-Celtic racism · 33

B

Bad water and disease · 131
beat complaint recording
    procedure · 84
Better Together · 151
Billet Master, Inspector of
    weights and measures, and
    Inspector of common
    lodgings · 86
Bishop of Durham · 7
Borough of Durham Reports
    of Inspectors of
    Constabulary · 85
Bourgeoisie · 21
branding emblem which says
    simply, 'Together' · 151

C

Case Studies · 70

Cleaning up the Poor · 116
Cohen's 'Folk Devils and
    Moral Panics' · 11
Common Lodging House Act
    · 91
complainant's addresses · 111
Complex social systems · 64
CONCLUSIONS · 140
confidential memorandum to
    Superintendents · 47
Cooter, 1972 · 25, 51
Counties Mayo, Roscommon,
    Sligo, Leitrim, and Galway ·
    67
County Mayo · 67
Court Records · 39
Crime and Disorder Act · 155
Crime and Disorder Act, 1998
    and Community Safety
    Partnerships · 157
Cultural Relic · 23
Culture Busters · 166

D

Darwin, 1871 · 32
de-institutionalising processes
    · 153
Deviance · 28
dialogical avowal · 155
disorder and violence caused
    at Witton Park, near Crook,
    · 52

Doctor Clarke · **120**

Dr. Clark had concluded · **131**

Dr. Watkin · **120**

Drs. Oliver and Watkin · **123**

Durham Chronicle · **26**

Durham City as a medicalizable object · **137**

Durham City Board of Health · **122**

Durham City Borough Police · **2, 76, 80, 82**

Durham City Borough Police during the period 1860 to 1871 · **82**

Durham City Borough Police, Superintendent's Annual Report 31.5.1876 · **90**

Durham City Council · **4**

Durham City Council Paving Commissioners' · **17**

Durham City Irish were well settled · **106**

Durham City Petty Sessional Court · **25**

Durham City Police Officers about 1850. · **89**

Durham City Town Hall · **37, 46**

Durham Constabulary, Aykley Heads, Durham City · **82**

Durham County Advertiser · **26**

Durham County Constabulary · **80**

Durham County Constabulary General Order Book. · **48**

Durham County Constabulary, Chief Constable's Reports of 1859 · **49**

Durham County Constabulary. · **47**

Durham Magistrates · **39**

E

Effectiveness and Efficiency · **77**

EPILOUGE. · **149**

F

Fear of Catholics · **31**

females apprehended · **81**

Fenianism and Disorder · **46**

Figure 1. The Stolen Altar Furniture · **3**

Finnigan, 1986 · **24**

Foucault · **18**

Foucault, 1975 · **16**

Framwellgate and Water Lane · **10**

Framwellgate and Water Lane in Elvet, were the unhealthiest areas of the City · **106**

Framwellgate Bridge in 1826 · **132**

G

General Orders of the force ·
92
Gidden's idea of De-
Institutionalisation and
'Cultural Relic' · 11
Giddens, Beck and Lash · 23
Grey Towers of Durham · 56

H

half church of God, half castle
against the Scot · 56
Health of Towns Association ·
114
horrifying tales of human
misery · 68

I

indictable offences · 81
Industrial Revolution · 37
INTRODUCING THE
PALATINATE, THE
PENINSULAR AND
THE SLUM · 6
Irish brawl · 49
Irish Defendants Indicted
before Durham Quarter
Sessions, 1867-1872 · 44
Irish immigrants who came to
the Northeast of England ·
65
Irish in York · 24

Irish jokes and Irish brawls ·
49
Irish matters in the Durham
Chronicle of 1871. · 51
Irish-born Population of
County Durham 1841-1881
· 38

J

J.C. Backhouse · 61
John Backhouse · 59
John Church Backhouse,
Banker · 59

L

Land of the Prince Bishops · 8
letter was printed from
Superintendent Robison ·
87
Lombroso, 1876 · 32
Lord de Freyne · 73
Lord Morpeth's economic
perception · 116

M

Marx and Engels · 21
McDonnell's study of the Irish
in Durham City between
1841 and 1861 · 66
McManus, 1989 · 105
McManus, 1995 · 80, 155

medicalisation of society · **7**
medicalization of spaces
    undertaken by lodging
    house keepers · **128**
minor beat complaint register ·
    84
monks of Lindisfarne · **56**
Moral Panic · **22**
Municipal Corporations Act ·
    79
Municipal Corporations Act
    1935 · **77**

N

New Localism and
    Neighbourhood Policing ·
    157
Number of Offences by Type
    committed by Irish and
    heard at Durham City Petty
    Sessional Court between
    1.1.1861 and   31.12.1861 ·
    42

P

P.C. Hart lost an eye · **53**
Pasquino · **19**
Pasquino 1978: 52 · **iv**
Pasquino, 1978 · **16**
Pasquino's 'science of police' ·
    10
Pasquino's conceptual, 'cluster
    of practices' · **115**

Peases', Darlington's most
    prominent Quaker family ·
    60
Peninsular of Durham City ·
    55
Peninsular Residents · **58**
persons categorized as
    servants · **57**
POLICE OF CRIME AND
    DISORDER · **76**
Police of Highways · **132**
POLICE OF PUBLIC
    UTILITES · **114**
*Police of Spaces. The medicalization
    and hygienic transformation of
    family life in Durham City* ·
    126
policing of dwellings · **122**
popular location for Irish
    immigrants · **37**
Population of County
    Durham, 1871 · **43**
Population of Durham City,
    1861 · **39**
primary culprits of minor
    complaints · **98**
problem of Fenianism · **47**
Proletariat · **21**

Q

Quaker banking family · **60**

R

Ragged Schools · **99**

Reflexive modernization · **152**

regulation of the population and the disciplining of the individual · **19**

Relics · **23**

Reporting on the causes of ill health in Durham City in 1853 · **116**

Respectable and loyal Irish assist the English Police · **36**

Responsibilization of the public · **155**

Richard Clarkson, Sergeant · **111**

Robert Ruddick · **94**

S

science of police · **117**

Scientific racism · **32**

Seven Highest Areas of Mortality by Street, 1841-1851 · **118**

Seven Lowest Areas of Mortality by Street, 1841-1851 · **75**

sewage facilities · **74**

shell institutions · **154**

Sir Robert Peel · **68**

Sir Robert Peel's 'New Police' · **17**

social classes of those who made complaints to the Durham City Police · **108**

St. Oswald's Church · i, **2**

Statistics and Power · **136**

Stereotyping the Irish · **26**

Street gambling · **79**

Superintendent Beard · **93**

Superintendent Beard to show a forceful management style · **92**

Superintendent William Robison · **85**

Surveillance · **20, 121**

Survival of Traditional Culture · **168**

T

tax-paying upper classes · **78**

the border with Scotland. · **56**

The Complainants · **103**

The Durham Directory of 1851 · **58**

The Irish Folk Devil · **27**

The Irish in Durham · **11**

The Media · **49**

The New Administration: The Science of Police · **16**

The Nuisance · **100**

The Palatinate of County Durham · **7**

THE PALATINATE: IRISH STEREOTYPING, CRIME · **24**

The Paving Committee · **74**

THE PENINSULAR · **55**

The Peninsular of Durham City · **9**

The Police of Public Utilities · **14**

The population of the Peninsular Parishes in 1851 · **56**

The register of minor complaints (the register) · **92**

the register' · **5**

the regulation of slaughterhouses · **131**

The Slum of Durham City · **10**

The Surveillance of Society · **144**

The Townland · **124**

The Veneration and Death of the Traditional Detective? · **160**

The Watched · **97**

The Watchers · **85**

Theoretical Interpretation · **10**

THEORETICAL INTERPRETATION: THE SCIENCE OF POLICE, MORAL PANIC AND CULTURAL RELIC · **15**

Those Charged before Durham City Petty Sessional Court between 1856-1861 · **41**

Time Travelling · **3**

Together · **150**

townland culture · **69**

Type and Number of Offences with which Irish were charged at Durham Quarter Sessions in 1871 · **45**

V

Voice From Thornley · **107**

W

Water Lane and Court Lane · **112**

William Beard · **90**

William Petty · **116**

William Robison · **86, 87**

William Robison (centre) Superintendent of Police Durham City 1848-57 · **88**

Williams, 1983 · **21**

Z

Zedner · **18**

Zombie Institutions · **157**

The Palatinate, The Peninsular and The Slum

ABOUT THE AUTHOR

Michael McManus was born in Durham City, UK in 1946. He is a Retired Airman, Royal Navy (1964-1971); Retired Police Officer, Durham Constabulary (1971-1999); Retired Part-time Teacher, University of Durham (1999-2015). He is married to Annette, for 55 years and they live in Durham City. He was awarded a BA (Hons) from the University of Northumbria and a Ph.D. from the University of Durham. He is now a Leisure Painter, Leisure Writer, and Leisure Poet.

Printed in Great Britain
by Amazon

35698732R00110